THE ART OF

Disney

Raya

AND

THE LAST DRAGON

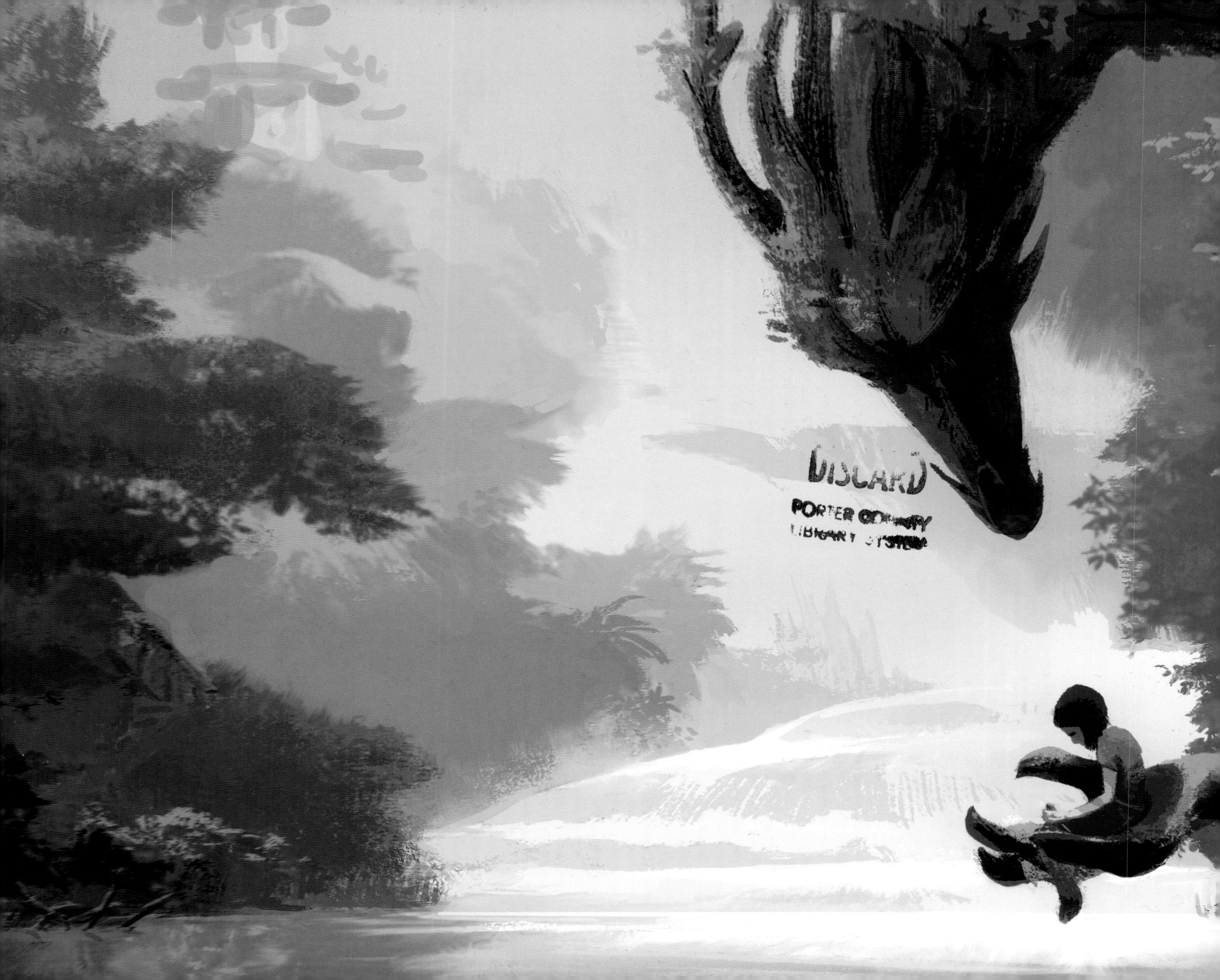

THE ART OF
Disney
RAYA
AND
THE LAST DRAGON

By **Kalikolehua Hurley** and **Osnat Shurer**

Foreword by **Don Hall, Carlos López Estrada,
Paul Briggs,** and **John Ripa**

CHRONICLE BOOKS
SAN FRANCISCO

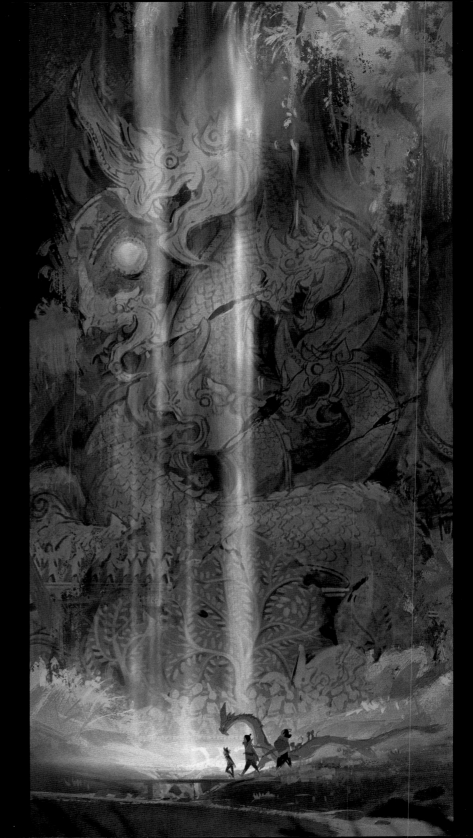

Creating a computer-generated animated film involves years of inspired collaboration. Before the final rendered images of *Raya* were seen on screens around the world, the following artists contributed their talents to the images included in this book:

Adam Levy, Adil Mustafabekov, Alberto Luceño Ros, Alena Loftis, Alex Garcia, Allan Bernardo, Allen Blaisdell, Andrea Paolino, Andrew Jennings, Angela McBride, Avneet Kaur, Becky Bresee, Benjamin Girmann, Benjamin Min Huang, Bobby Huth, Brandon Lawless, Brent Homman, Brian Leach, Brian Missey, Cameron Black, Chad Stubblefield, Chaiwon Kim, Chantal LeBlanc, Charles Scott, Chris Nabholz, Christoffer Pedersen, Christopher Evart, Christopher Hendryx, Daniel Klug, Daniel Kole, David Suroviec, Deborah Carlson, Derek Nelson, Diana J. LeVangiel, D'Lun Wong, Don Taylor, Dylan Ekren, Dylan VanWormer, Eric Provan, Erik Eulen, Erik Hansen, Foam Laohachaiaroon, Garrett Eves, Henrik Falt, Holly Kim-Angel, Hubert Leo, Ian Butterfield, Iker J. de los Mozos, Iva Itchevska-Brain, Jack Geckler, Jacqueline Koehler, Jason Robinson, Jason Stellwag, Jean-Cristophe Poulain, Jeff Chung, Jennifer Hager, Jennifer Stratton, Jesus Canal, Jim Finn, Joan Anastas, Joaquin Baldwin, Johann Francois Coetzee, John Murrah, Jongo Yuk, Joseph Piercy, Josh Fry, Joshua Slice, Juan Pablo Chen, Kaori Doi, Kate Kirby-O'Connell, Kelley Williams, Kelsey Grier, Kendra Vander Vliet, Kevin Lee, Kevin MacLean, Ki Jong Hong, Kim Hazel, Konrad Lightner, Kori Amacker, Ksenia Bezrukov, Lance Summers, Larry Wu, Laura H. Han, Lindsey St. Pierre, Mack Kablan, Malerie Walters, Marc Thyng, Mario Furmanczyk, Mark Empey, Masha Zarnitsa, Mathew Thomas, Matt Lee, Matthew Schiller, Merrick Rustia, Michael Altman, Michael Cheng, Michael Morris, Michael Talarico, Michael W. Stieber, Mike Navarro, Minh Duong, Mitch Snary, Nathan Dillow, Nicklas Puetz, Nikki Mull, Pamela Spertus, Paul Carman, Pedro Garcia Perez, Punn Wiantrakoon, Rattanin Sirinaruemarn, Rich Fallat, Richard Van Cleave, Rick Moore, Rob Dressel, Robert Bennett, Robert L. Miles, Ryan DeYoung, Samy Segura, Sergi Cabeller Garcia, Shaun Absher, Si-Hyung Kim, Solhee Ryu, Steve Null, Suan Tan, Sung Joon Bae, SuZan Kim, Tammy Kersavage, Terry Moews, Tim J. Richards, Tim Molinder, Tony Bonilla, Travis Mangaoang, Tyler Kupferer, Vicky Lin, Virgilio John Aquino, Xinmin Zhao, Zack Petroc

Library of Congress Cataloging-in-Publication Data available.

ISBN: 978-1-7972-0725-4

Manufactured in Italy

FSC
www.fsc.org

MIX
Paper from
responsible sources
FSC® C127663

Design by Jennifer Redding and Neil Egan.

(Cover) **Mingjue Helen Chen:** Digital
(Front Flap) **Ami Thompson:** Digital
(Endsheets) **Mingjue Helen Chen:** Digital
(Page 1) **Paul Felix:** Digital
(Pages 2-3) **Kevin Nelson:** Digital
(This Page) **Mingjue Helen Chen:** Digital

10 9 8 7 6 5 4 3 2 1

Chronicle Books LLC
680 Second Street
San Francisco, California 94107
www.chroniclebooks.com

CONTENTS

Paul Felix: Digital

FOREWORD

—BY DON HALL, CARLOS LÓPEZ ESTRADA, PAUL BRIGGS, AND JOHN RIPA

EVERY WALT DISNEY ANIMATION STUDIOS FILM is both a labor of love and an act of daring bravery. It begins with an idea and then takes a confluence of amazing artists, designers, and technicians to bring it to reality. And as many times as we've done this, it always feels like magic once we can finally share the film with audiences.

To achieve this, it takes more than just talent and hard work; it takes trust. From the first words on the page to the very last detail added before our film premieres to the world, every step along our journey requires each of us to reach out and hold each other up, especially during times when the circumstances are the most challenging. Trust is both the theme of our movie and the secret ingredient that makes all our films possible. And, honestly, there is nothing we'd rather offer the world today.

This theme of trust permeated every aspect in the making of *Raya and the Last Dragon*. It started when our teams visited Thailand, Vietnam, Cambodia, Laos, Indonesia, Malaysia, and Singapore, where we were continually inspired by the warmth and generosity of the people we met and the cultural insights they shared with us. This collaboration continued unbroken as our teams returned to the studio and held ongoing conversations and story sessions with members of our Southeast Asia Story Trust to ensure that *Raya*, although an original fantasy story, continues to honor its Southeast Asian roots.

Our ambition with this film was to create characters and a world unlike any we've ever seen before in the already legendary canon of Disney Animation films. That's no easy task. What we asked from our artists was the stars. What they gave us in return was a universe—one filled with timeless characters, incredible landscapes, and lovable creatures. We are absolutely humbled by each and every one of them and their remarkable artistry.

It's been a long journey from the genesis of this idea until now. The film you see is the result of the talent, craft, expertise, and, most of all, commitment of so many. It takes an amazing collective effort to realize something of this magnitude.

This book is a tribute to all the talented artists who have made this journey with us, from visual development and story to cinematography, characters, environments, set extension, animation, effects, and beyond, and to everyone at Disney Animation. We feel honored to have shared the journey of *Raya and the Last Dragon* with you. Even when we had to work from our separate homes during the COVID-19 pandemic of 2020, we were, and are, united in every frame of this film.

INTRODUCTION

RAYA AND THE LAST DRAGON is an original fantasy, action-adventure film, set in a world inspired by the cultures and people of Southeast Asia.

As the filmmakers traveled through Laos, Vietnam, Cambodia, Thailand, Singapore, Malaysia, and Indonesia, they experienced magnificent architecture, exquisite art, and gorgeous landscapes. They listened, and they learned. The sense of acceptance, unity, and trust they encountered resonated deeply with their own experiences and helped inspire the themes of the film.

The conversations that were initiated with storytellers, historians, anthropologists, architects, linguists, textile experts, master dancers, and musicians evolved into an ongoing collaboration that continued throughout production. The Southeast Asia Story Trust, as they collectively became known, helped inspire and inform the film from environment and character design to story and animation.

Raya *is* a princess. She is the daughter of the chief of the Heart Lands. She is also a fierce warrior whose wit is as sharp as her blade. While creating a period piece, the filmmakers wanted to make the world feel contemporary and full of color, taking constant sharp turns into surprising action and humor.

The bigger philosophical questions the movie asks are important to the filmmakers and are timely, as well as timeless. Its hero, Raya, believes that "in a broken world, you cannot trust anyone," while her father, Chief Benja of Heart, and Sisu, the last dragon, believe that "the world is broken because you don't trust anyone."

These opposing philosophies inform the journey of the movie. Kumandra, the epic world in which the story takes place, was once one land, one people, living in harmony with the dragons. But the dragons are gone, and Kumandra has fractured into five distinct, hostile lands representing the five parts of the dragon: Heart, Tail, Talon, Spine, and Fang. Each character that Raya meets along the way represents one of the lands of Kumandra. Each, in turn, pushes on the central theme of trust.

The artists approached designing the lands by exploring how each region's distinct characteristics and personalities could be expressed through its climate, geography, materials, and design aesthetics. Then, in collaboration with the Southeast Asia Story Trust, the designers applied a Southeast Asian cultural lens to the designs.

The result is the art of the fantasy world of Kumandra.

Kevin Nelson: Digital

(previous spread) **Paul Felix:** Digital

(this page) **Paul Felix:** Digital

(next spread) **Brittney Lee,
Mingjue Helen Chen, and
Griselda Sastrawinata:** Digital

PROLOGUE

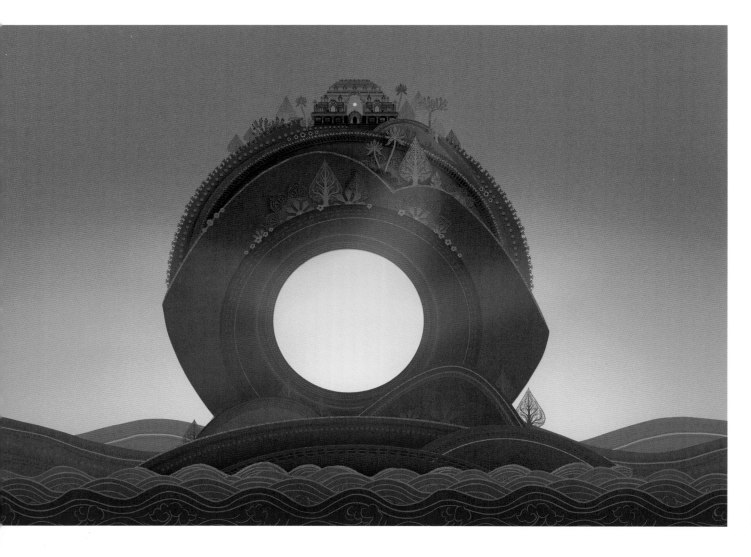

Brittney Lee and Mingjue Helen Chen: Digital

RAYA AND THE LAST DRAGON begins with a story, recounted by the film's titular character, Raya:

"Kumandra. This is what we used to be, when our land was whole and we lived harmoniously with dragons—magical creatures who brought us water and rain and peace. It was paradise.

"But then the Druun came, a mindless plague, multiplying as they consumed life and turning everyone they touched into stone. The dragons fought for us the best they could, but it wasn't enough.

"That's when the mighty Sisudatu, the last dragon, concentrated all her magic into a gem and blasted the Druun away. Everyone that was turned to stone came back, except the dragons.

"All that was left of Sisu was her gem.

"It should have been this big inspirational moment where humanity united over her sacrifice, but instead—people being people—they all fought to possess the last remnant of dragon magic. Borders were drawn. Kumandra divided. We all became enemies. And the gem had to be hidden.

"But that's not how the world broke. Nope. That didn't truly happen until five hundred years later when I came into the story."

Griselda Sastrawinata: Digital

Mingjue Helen Chen: Digital

PART 1
A WARRIOR AND A DRAGON

R AYA BEGINS HER JOURNEY in *Raya and the Last Dragon* as a twelve-year-old warrior-in-training. Smart and determined, she passes her final test and joins her beloved father, Benja, chief of the Heart Lands, as a Guardian of the sacred Dragon Gem. But soon they are betrayed, and tragedy strikes. The Gem breaks, unleashing the terrible Druun, who turn Benja to stone. Shattered by her loss, Raya sets off on a tireless search for Sisu, the last dragon, whom she believes is the only hope to bring her father back. After six solitary years of searching, Raya finally finds Sisu. But they soon discover that without the Gem, Sisu is powerless. Together they must journey through hostile lands to find all of the pieces of the Gem and save the world.

"The core of our story has always been Raya and Sisu," reveals director Don Hall. "The interplay between their different personalities—one a warrior with trust issues and the other a benevolent dragon who trusts deeply—is the source of not just the film's humor, but also its emotion." For producer Osnat Shurer, the duo's status as heroines made their storytelling potential all the more exciting. "We jumped at the opportunity to develop not one but two strong, nuanced, extraordinary female characters," she recalls fondly.

Early on, the visual development team explored designs for Raya and Sisu on separate tracks, yielding a rich array of diverse shape and look options for each character, including Sisu as a dragon and in her human form. But something was missing. "We realized that we couldn't design either of these characters individually without first visualizing them together," says co-director Paul Briggs.

"At the core of our film are two characters, their arc, and their relationship," says art director of characters Shiyoon Kim, "so I tried to imagine the two of them at different moments in their journey." Kim sketched the two as pals who hang out and share secrets, "growing closer and opening up over time." He drew them like opposites from a buddy comedy film, "with one stoic and the other comedic," and in antagonistic moments where they're fighting, "hilariously, of course." Kim found the approach an unusual

(previous spread) **Paul Felix:** Digital

Scott Watanabe: Digital

Ami Thompson: Digital

Shiyoon Kim: Digital

challenge. "Typically, I'm comparing shapes against shapes, like 'the shape of this character could look great next to this shape of this other character.' But here, regardless of what was happening shape-wise, we really needed the audience to believe that these two characters could go on this journey together."

Kim's efforts paid off. "Out of the blue," remembers director, pre-production Dean Wellins, "Shiyoon put up a bunch of images he drew, including one where Raya had Sisu, who unbeknownst to Raya was actually a dragon, pinned against a wall. We lost it!" Production designer Paul Felix agrees. "At that time in our story, Raya was a no-nonsense swordswoman focused on her goal: to find Sisu and bring her father back. Sisu, on the

other hand, was the dragon Raya had been searching for but was trapped in her human form and refused to cooperate or give Raya a straight answer. Shiyoon summed up that exasperated relationship between the two of them really nicely."

From then on, co-director John Ripa clarifies, the story evolved dramatically. Raya softened, and Sisu began her journey in the film as a magnificent dragon full of hope and helpfulness. "Still," he chuckles, "we held on to the fun idea that Raya drives in a straight line and Sisu does nothing in a straight line—everything is sideways, even when she's trying to be helpful. And you can imagine how that might feel to someone who is trying to get something done."

RAYA

RAYA IS, and has always been, a warrior. "Raya was forced to leave her home early in the story," muses director Carlos López Estrada, "and had to learn to raise herself in order to survive." "But warrior characters can be hard to relate to," director Don Hall continues, "so we had to balance Raya's tough exterior with many rich layers of personality."

Raya is athletic and fit, and her fighting acumen is second-to-none. She is tall, five-eight, with an impressive presence. Her braid "keeps her hair out of the way," explains production designer Paul Felix.

Research in Southeast Asia inspired Raya's look. "We wanted her features to have an observed quality that felt authentic to people from the region," says Shiyoon Kim, art director of characters. Cultural specificity was achieved by focusing on subtlety and, Kim adds, the artistry of character modeling supervisor Alena Loftis. "Raya has a gorgeous eye shape, a soft, feminine nose, and strong, prominent cheekbones, all qualities sculpted in CG," Loftis recounts. "She's stunning."

Functionality is a key aspect of Raya's clothing. "Raya is a swordswoman," says costume designer Neysa Bové, "so we thought of outfitting her in leather, which protects the skin and stretches with movement." But much of Kumandra is tropical, and an all-leather outfit was not practical. "It'd be way too hot," she laughs. So the team looked to the more breathable draping styles of the region, including the *sabai* top and *dhoti* pants, and landed on a combination of the two. Bové continues, "Raya's fluid top and pant paired with her leather boots and jacket provide an overall structured silhouette that allow her to move in a believable way."

Story development also influenced Raya's costume. Over time, she became more distrustful. "We added a cape with a high collar and a large hat that she could hide under—her protective layers, items we could peel away as she evolves with the film," co-director John Ripa explains. Designed in collaboration with Lao visual anthropologist Dr. Soulinhakhath Steve Arounsack, the slope of Raya's hat ascends to a sacred peak—an homage to *stupas* found at temples in the region.

"Ultimately, our Raya is a strong, resilient, and quick-witted warrior with a sharp sense of humor," exclaims co-director Paul Briggs. "She's a total badass."

Shiyoon Kim: Digital

Ami Thompson: Digital

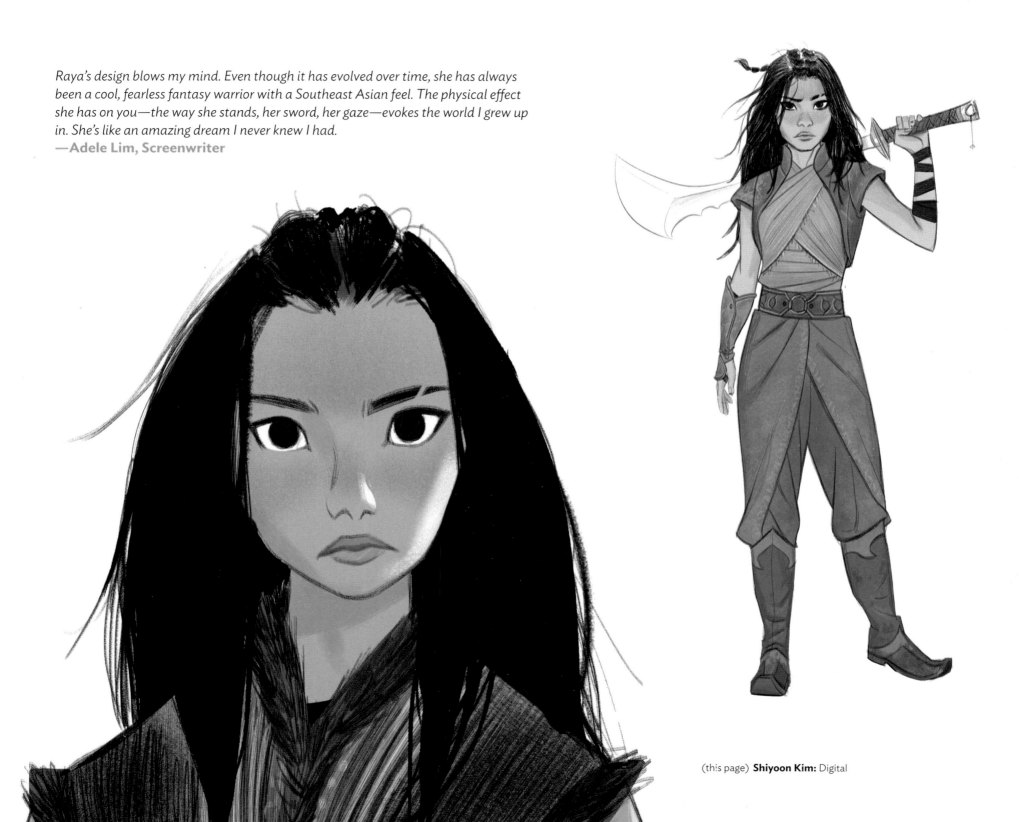

Raya's design blows my mind. Even though it has evolved over time, she has always been a cool, fearless fantasy warrior with a Southeast Asian feel. The physical effect she has on you—the way she stands, her sword, her gaze—evokes the world I grew up in. She's like an amazing dream I never knew I had.
—Adele Lim, Screenwriter

(this page) **Shiyoon Kim:** Digital

Malcon Pierce (pose) and Shiyoon Kim (drawover): Digital

Malcon Pierce: Digital

Raya is a character with trust issues and the weight of the world on her shoulders. Her task is monumental—to bring back her father and save the world. It would be easy to play her as closed off and sulky, but we knew that wouldn't work. We wanted her to be very expressive and experience a wide range of emotions. To that end, we focused on finding Raya's fun and comedic side in all of her scenes. The end result is a believable, multilayered character who, like all of us, has room to grow. —Malcon Pierce, Head of Animation

Griselda Sastrawinata: Digital

Neysa Bové: Digital

Raya's costume is a nod to her upbringing in Heart, the land that most reveres the auspicious dragons. If you look closely, you'll see hints of the dragon and raindrops, the motif of Heart, everywhere. Her pants are printed with a stylized dragon pattern, and her jacket has an embossed texture that represents raindrops. Dragon scales are carved into the tip of her hat. Even her cloak is embroidered with dragon shapes, and its lining printed with little raindrops. —**Neysa Bové, Costume Designer**

Neysa Bové: Digital

Raya has soft, feminine features. She also has a sharpness to her. The combination of the two gives her a strength we do not always see in animated female characters. This mix of subtle details really pushes her into another realm.
—Alena Loftis, Character Modeling Supervisor

Neysa Bové: Digital

Alena Loftis (model) and Various Artists: CG Render

Raya's sword is a fantastical take on an ancient dagger called the kris or keris from Indonesia. Like a smartphone, it is high tech. Twisting the handle extends the blade in an unexpected way, allowing Raya to grab or hook onto things, or even change direction when she is riding her trusty steed, Tuk Tuk.
—Mehrdad Isvandi, Visual Development Artist

Ami Thompson: Digital

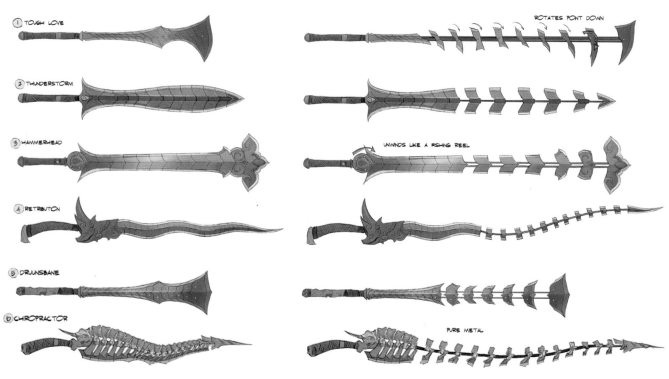

① TOUGH LOVE

② THUNDERSTORM

③ HAMMERHEAD

④ RETRIBUTION

⑤ DRUMSBANE

⑥ CHIROPRACTOR

ROTATES POINT DOWN

UNWINDS LIKE A FISHING REEL

PURE METAL

Cory Loftis: Digital

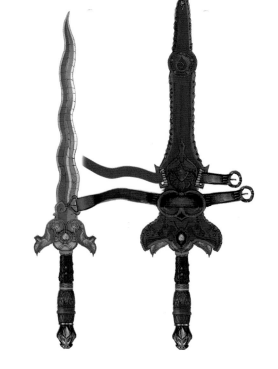

Mehrdad Isvandi: Digital

Exploring the design for Raya's weapons was a lot of fun. As a character, she's really smart. She knows her tactics and in previous versions of the story even made her own fantasy weapons. I thought of things I hadn't ever seen before, like a bunch of bells she could drag that could attract or distract the baddies or a customized arm cannon that could fire off spark balls to stun them.

—**Ami Thompson, Art Director of Characters**

USE SPARKS TO BLIND THEM

(this page) **Ami Thompson:** Digital

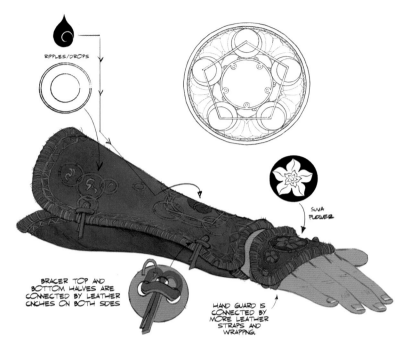

RIPPLES/DROPS

BRACER TOP AND
BOTTOM HALVES ARE
CONNECTED BY LEATHER
CINCHES ON BOTH SIDES

HAND GUARD IS
CONNECTED BY
MORE LEATHER
STRAPS AND
WRAPPING.

SUVA
FLOWER

Cory Loftis: Digital

(above and below) **Ami Thompson:** Digital

*In the film, Raya is a skilled fighter. She's also
ambidextrous. Her hand-to-hand style of fighting
is inspired by* Pencak Silat *from Indonesia
and* Muay Thai, *and her weapons style is
inspired by* Arnis, *also known as* Kali, *from the
Philippines.* —**Qui Nguyen, Screenwriter**

(this page) **Ami Thompson:** Digital

RUN!!!

YOUNG RAYA

Ami Thompson: Digital

(this page) **Ami Thompson:** Digital

As they say, you can't be what you can't see. I'm so grateful that we get to put out into the world strong, aspirational characters that will mean so much to people that look like me and my kids. As an Asian American, I wish I'd had a superhero like Raya when I was small. I hope she inspires my children as much as my favorite superheroes inspired me.
—Qui Nguyen, Screenwriter

April Liu: Digital

Ami Thompson: Digital

Young Raya's costume is fit for a princess. Its draped silhouette is constructed from rich, woven silk and brocade—exquisite fabrics often associated with royalty in Southeast Asia— with a gold-threaded raindrop pattern. She is adorned with an arm cuff and a little metal ring on her shoulder that is a double-headed dragon. Her lustrous jacket is embellished with rain clouds and a dragon wrapped around her collar.
—Neysa Bové, Costume Designer

Ami Thompson: Digital

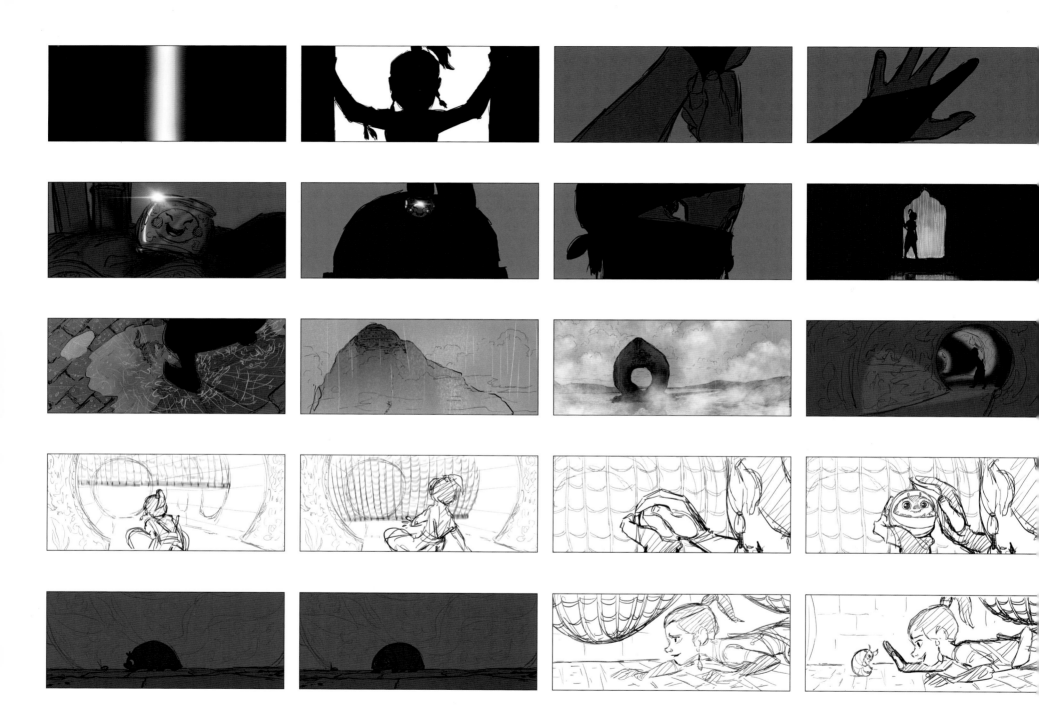

John Ripa: Digital

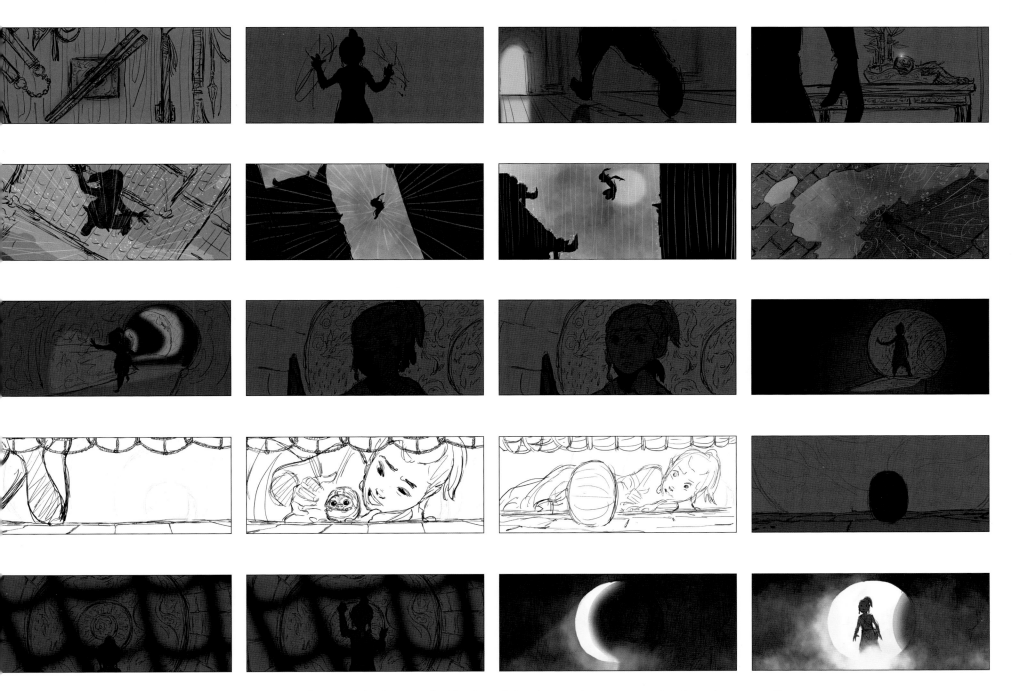

When co-director John Ripa pitched his boards for the opening sequence that introduces us to Raya and her father, Benja, we were all so excited because we knew immediately that this was exactly what our film needed. The tone, pacing, and camera in this sequence inform that of the whole film. It was brilliant and so much fun to cut! —**Fabienne Rawley, Editor**

TUK TUK

Part pill bug, part pug, part pangolin, part high-speed off-road vehicle, and all adorable, Tuk Tuk has been Raya's best friend since she could hold him in the palm of her hand. Now they are both grown, and Tuk Tuk is Raya's faithful, gigantic steed. Together they tear through the varied terrains of Kumandra at incredible speeds on a journey to restore the last dragon and save the world.
—**Paul Briggs, Co-director**

Ami Thompson: Digital

Mingjue Helen Chen: Digital

Scott Watanabe: Digital

Ami Thompson: Digital

Tuk Tuk was born from the very unique sensibility of visual development artist Scott Watanabe. Like all fantasy action-adventure heroes, Raya needed a super cool ride. We talked about using pill bugs and doodlebugs as inspiration, and on the first pass Scott came back to us with these images. We thought, "That's Tuk Tuk!" —**Dean Wellins, Director, Pre-production**

Ami Thompson: Digital

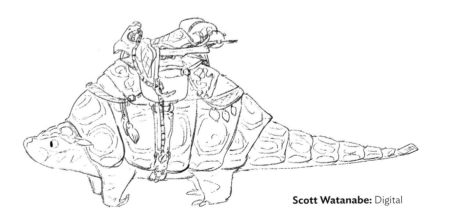

Scott Watanabe: Digital

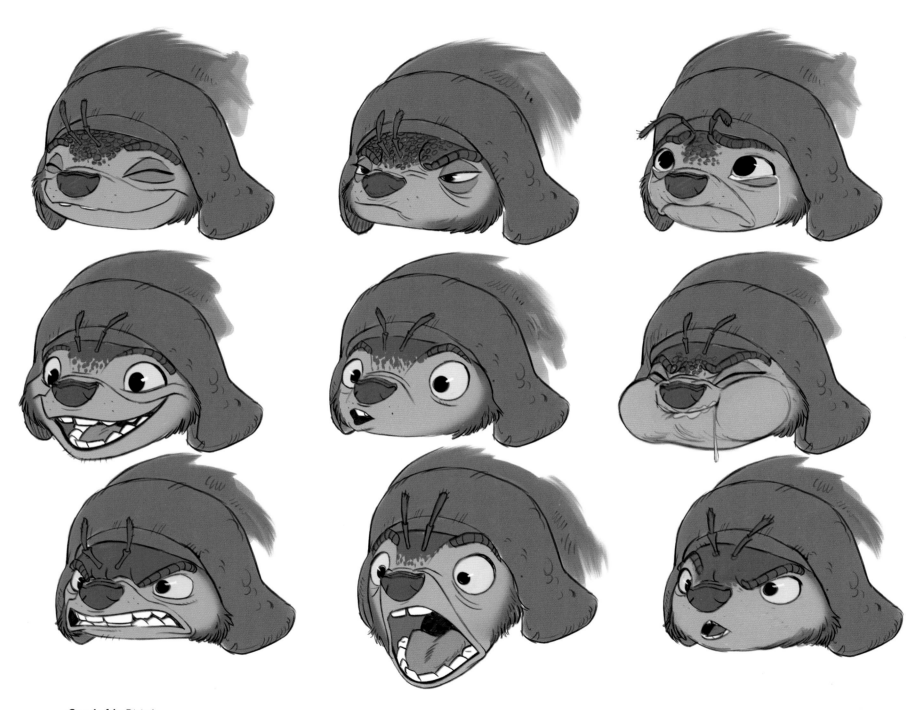

Cory Loftis: Digital

Cory Loftis: Digital

When the story called for a baby version of Tuk Tuk, production designer Cory Loftis whipped up this tiny, furry ball of love, and it took an extraordinary amount of discipline not to turn the film into Baby Tuk Tuk and the Last Dragon. —**Don Hall, Director**

Fawn Veerasunthorn: Digital

SISU

SISU IS A WATER DRAGON inspired by the *naga*—powerful, mythical beings of Southeast Asia who are often able to manifest as serpent or human and are usually associated with bodies of water. "Sisu is an eternal optimist," declares director Carlos López Estrada, "a wise sage who teaches Raya about the power of trust and unity. But, after being asleep for five hundred years, she also has a lot to learn about contemporary life."

Designing an enigmatic, wise, and powerful fantasy dragon rooted in Southeast Asian inspiration was an exciting challenge for the team. "Our goal was for Sisu to be so inspiring visually that someone might even be moved to write poetry about her," art director of characters Shiyoon Kim recalls. The early exploration of Sisu included many different silhouettes and attitudes, from the ethereal and magical to the ferocious and skeptical.

"Sisu's design went through a lot of starts and stops," says Cory Loftis, production designer. "The first place many of us would go was high-fantasy Western dragon with bat wings and scales, so we really had to do our research." Producer Osnat Shurer credits close collaboration with the film's Southeast Asia Story Trust for the fine-tuning of Sisu so that she could remain fantastical and unique to the world while also being respectful of regional customs and beliefs. "We are especially grateful to have worked with Lao visual anthropologist Dr. S. Steve Arounsack and Thai architect Nathakrit Tatan Sunthareerat on our journey to create Sisu."

Visualizing Sisu was a thrill for head of story Fawn Veerasunthorn, who grew up in Thailand. "At home, the *naga* are a significant part of everyday life. They are designed into our architecture and stand guard at our temples. Their powerful presence creates a feeling that they actually exist in an invisible world of which we are not a part. We explored that concept in Kumandra, where the dragons were once revered, and similarly reflected their shape everywhere. The moment Raya discovers that there is a living dragon in her world must be a pretty amazing one for her."

(this spread) **Paul Felix:** Digital

SISU DRAGON

(this page) **Scott Watanabe:** Digital

We anchored Sisu's design and spiritual essence in regional naga mythologies. For example, the prominence and elevation of the crest along with a serpentine body were central design features. Sisu's design is personal for me because my people revere the naga and her life-affirming philosophies. We thought through all the beautiful and meaningful ways to enshrine our beloved water dragon for generations to come.
—**Dr. S. Steve Arounsack, Visual Anthropologist, Southeast Asia Story Trust**

Shiyoon Kim: Digital

Paul Felix: Digital

Sisu's rich blue tone ties her to water. Her fins and the S-curve shape of her body show that she's an excellent swimmer. Her crest, a signature trait of the naga that we incorporated into her design, has on it a water-like motif unique to the world of Kumandra. Purple and pink in her luscious, full head of hair make her feel youthful, magical, and regal.
—**Ami Thompson, Art Director of Characters**

Ami Thompson: Digital

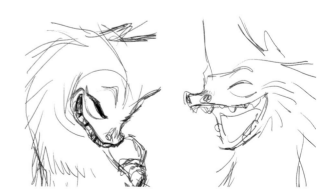

Shiyoon Kim: Digital

Ami Thompson: Digital

Sisu's animation style is a lot of fun and very entertaining! She is full of personality. I love what Awkwafina has brought to her voice, and the animation team had a blast animating her. When we first meet Sisu, she's full of comical moments, but as we get to know her through the film, we see a lot of depth to her character. She's a sincere optimist and sometimes a little naive. My favorite trait of hers is how she always thinks the best of people. —**Amy Smeed, Head of Animation**

Creating the magnificent Sisu in CG was an epic technical challenge for our characters team. Her unique, otherworldly form was incredibly complex to rig, and her fluid shape needed to perform as bipedal and quadrupedal. She really pushed the limits of our understanding of animation. —**Carlos Cabral, Head of Characters and Technical Animation**

Various Artists: CG Render

SISU HUMAN

We always imagined in the story room that Sisu would be terribly uncomfortable as a dragon in a human form. Her oversized clothes, especially those huge sleeves, say it all. —**John Ripa, Co-director**

(this page) **Shiyoon Kim:** Digital

Shiyoon Kim: Digital

We wanted to see a little bit of Sisu Dragon in her human form. The details of her coat include motifs that you also see in her dragon hide. The frays on the bottom of her jacket are very reminiscent of her fins. She even has a long sash that's reminiscent of her dragon tail.
—**Cory Loftis, Production Designer**

Neysa Bové: Digital

DRAGON EXPLORATION

Ami Thompson: Digital

The poses of the stone dragons were designed in close collaboration with our Southeast Asia Story Trust. The art and architecture of Southeast Asia imbue dragons and naga with meaning in the way they are positioned in protective poses along the rooflines of temples and palaces. The team wanted to capture that sense of majesty and awe for the film's audience, taking care to depict their power, elegance, and grace, and placing them in elevated locations high in the air.
—Scott Sakamoto, **Production Supervisor**

Zac Retz: Digital

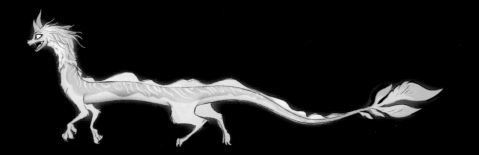

SISU SIBLINGS

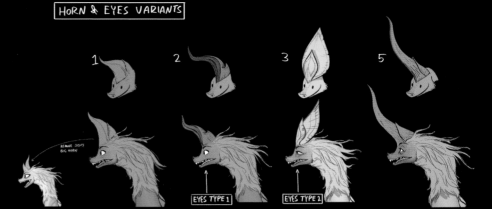

HORN & EYES VARIANTS

1 2 3 5

REMOVE SISU'S BIG HORN!

EYES TYPE 1   EYES TYPE 2

Ami Thompson: Digital

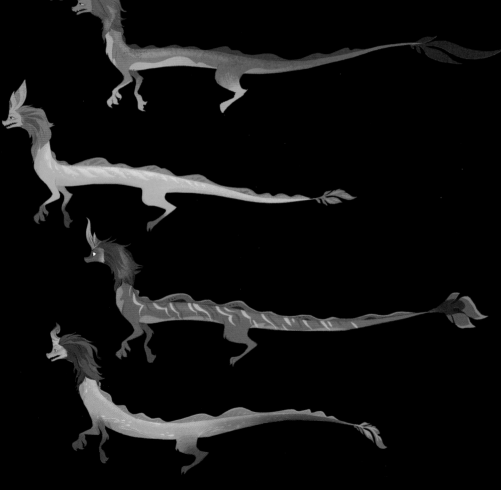

Ami Thompson: Digital

Our dragons are related to water, and we wanted to find a way to mark their footsteps as they push off raindrops. We landed on these colorful, refracted ripples of light.
— **Mingjue Helen Chen, Production Designer**

Mingjue Helen Chen: Digital

51

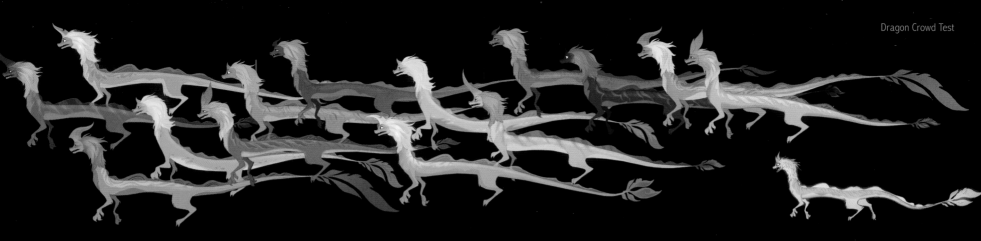

Crowd Dragon Variant #3

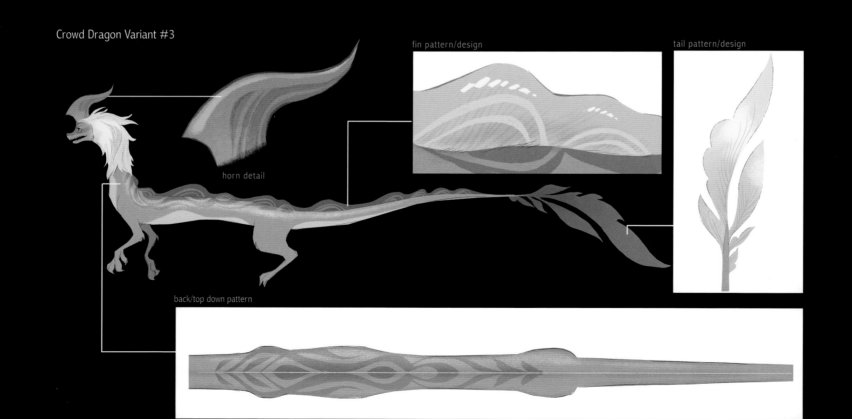

horn detail

fin pattern/design

tail pattern/design

back/top down pattern

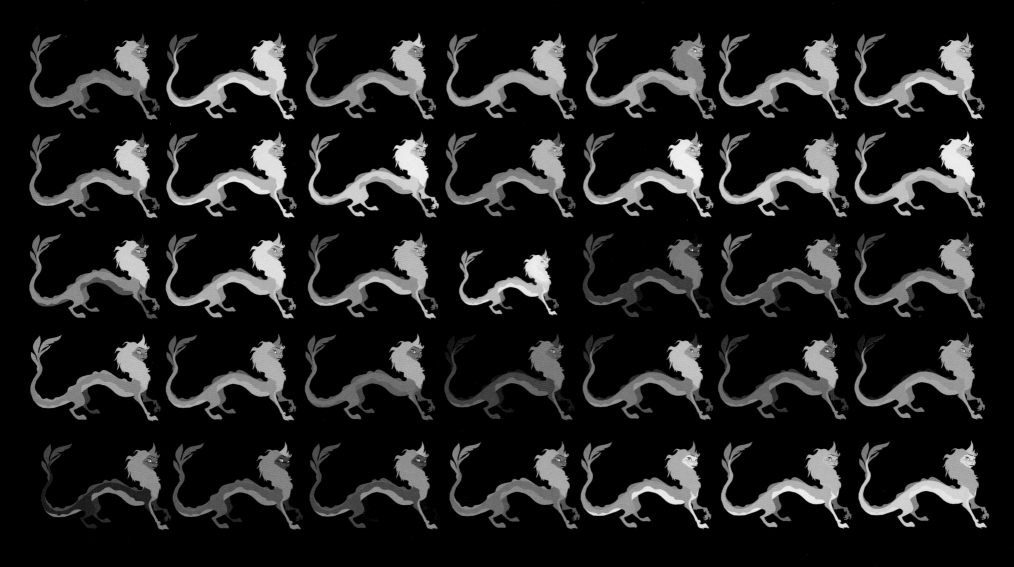

Our dragons need to look magical but feel believable in our world. In the look department, for inspiration we referenced a variety of beings with scales, translucent fins, fur, and skin that changed color. Our dragons also glow, and their grooms and textures needed to be fluid as their flexible bodies twisted and turned. As a result of much cross-departmental collaboration, we landed on a design that looks amazing and holds up to the performance. —**Nikki Mull, Character Look Supervisor**

(this spread) **Brittney Lee:** Digital

THE DRAGON GEM

Hundreds of years ago, the last dragons infused the Dragon Gem with their magic and power in a bid to protect humanity from the dreaded Druun, then vanished. Only the Dragon Gem remained, protected by generations of Guardians in the lands of Heart.
—**Carlos López Estrada, Director**

Mingjue Helen Chen: Digital

Mehrdad Isvandi: Digital

Mingjue Helen Chen: Digital

We used a lot of real-world reference for the Dragon Gem. We visited the gem collection at a natural history museum, researched and photographed all sorts of precious stones, including quartz, fluorite, and opals. The Dragon Gem needed to look made, not just found, but not perfectly polished like a diamond. It also lights up, so we lit the gems and added stage fog to see how the light would refract through it. The opals broke up the light in a beautiful spectrum of colors.
—Adolph Lusinsky, Director of Cinematography–Lighting

Benjamin Min Huang and Various Artists: Look Render

FANG

TALON

HEART

SPINE

PART 2
THE DRAGONLANDS

TAIL

RAYA AND THE LAST DRAGON takes place in the fictional world of Kumandra, a once united society now fractured into five lands situated along the Dragon River: Heart, Tail, Talon, Spine, and Fang.

Production designer Paul Felix was delighted to take on the challenge of designing five distinct lands with different climates and characteristics. "We knew we wanted the design of each land to visually reflect the personality of its people, as well as the geography, topography, and climate of its location around the Dragon River. And this was no small feat." For production designer Mingjue Helen Chen, it was a daunting dream project. "Sometimes it felt like we were making five movies instead of one," she marvels.

Felix and Chen first approached design by exploring the psychological makeup and outlook of each land. "A society that fights many wars will have different expectations from its architecture compared to a trading society," explains Felix. "With that line of thinking, it was easy for us to imagine how different priorities expressed themselves in city layout, color palette, and even ornaments."

A distinct personality emerged for each of the five lands. "Heart is aspirational and hopeful," director Don Hall reveals. "It's an island surrounded by water, the element of the ancient revered dragons in which the people of Heart still deeply believe." "Tail, the most geographically remote, is free-form and structureless, a desert haven for outliers and scavengers," offers director Carlos López Estrada. "Talon," notes co-director Paul Briggs, "is bustling and chaotic, full of merchants and traders vying for attention to make a buck." "Spine, located in a dramatic giant black bamboo forest on a snowy mountainside, is insular and defensive," says co-director John Ripa. Finally, adds Briggs, "Fang is all about power. They ascribe to the belief that 'might is right' and even live on a manufactured island of their own creation."

Back in design, the team translated these personalities into a visual narrative and unique aesthetic for each land. Heart took on a blue color palette with its motifs suggesting fluid water shapes. Tail's makeshift, dust-covered architecture leveraged found objects and scrap materials.

Loud, flashy Talon became full of layers of bright, bold, and colorful patterns. Fortifications dominated in Spine, with defensive spikes and weapon imagery. And Fang's ferocity was reinforced in the repetition of strong, bold, and sharp geometric shapes.

Next, the team looked to shared underlying design principles in Southeast Asia for inspiration. One of these main principles, producer Osnat Shurer explains, is that everything is rooted in, and centered around, a belief system or cosmology. "Visually, we represented Kumandran cosmology in general, and of each land in particular, through icons inspired by the *mandala*, a unique geometric configuration of symbols that often informs architectural designs of temples in places like Indonesia, Thailand, and Cambodia." "The icon for Heart," expounds Chen, "represents the round Dragon Gem, as well as radiating ripples of raindrops, yet another visual connection to Kumandra's dragon mythology." Fang, which is philosophically at odds with Heart, has an icon "full of squares." Talon's icon conveys the feeling of an explosion, "where everything is connected with dots, very spiderweb-y." Spine's icon looks like "the inside of a bamboo." Last, far-flung Tail has an icon that reflects a place where "everything is a little bit scattered." These icons also became the basis for each land's city or village layout.

Together, the five lands are represented in a five-pointed pentagon shape that is repeated in textile designs, city layouts, building shapes, costumes, and prop elements throughout the film. "This configuration visually represents how everything in our fictional world revolves around the five lands and their balance with each another," says production designer Cory Loftis.

Another way Kumandra's design visually communicates each land's connection to its central belief system is through temple design. Led by Chen, the approach focuses on the personality of each land and its available resources. "Heart, as we've established, is deeply spiritual and connected to the dragon, so we used a lot of round shapes and leaned into the idea of a raindrop coming down and creating ripples. Tail, on the other hand, is very minimal. Its people don't create over-the-top structures, so their temple is built out of the side of a mountain so subtly, it's barely noticeable."

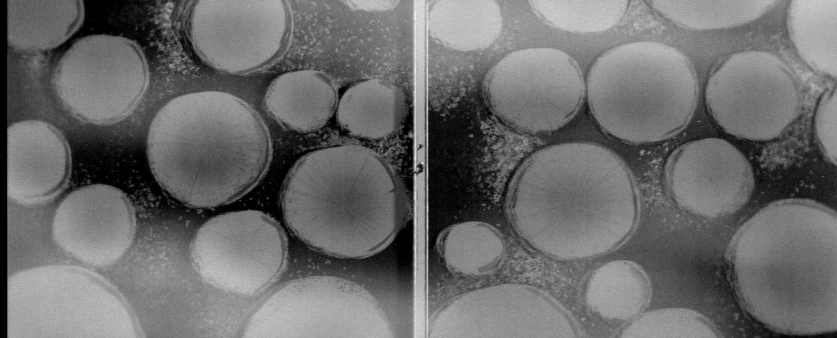

(this page)
Mingjue Helen Chen:
Digital

The time period of the film—set sometime between the ninth and twelfth centuries—also heavily influenced design. "Without modern construction methods, everything would've been handcrafted and would've looked slightly irregular and imperfect," says Felix, "so we had to pay close attention to materials, spacing, and consistency." Based on personality traits, each land was assigned a level of how "handmade" its construction would be. As head of environments Larry Wu notes, "Fang's construction is the most meticulous, followed by Heart, then Spine, Talon, and finally Tail."

Fantasy was also top of mind during the team's world-building process. After all, "Kumandra is a world where magic still exists and fantastical creatures roam," says Loftis. "We didn't want the audience to see these things as being out of place, so our world needed to be built with a sense of fantasy in every detail." To find fantasy, Loftis challenged the teams to surprise the audience by adding the unexpected, like using unfamiliar shapes and playing with scale and color. "We could take something that is known, for example, and place it in an unexpected location, like corals in the desert or cacti in the snow."

Soon, the team developed an impressive catalog of fantasy foliage, creating over two hundred variations of plants, shrubs, and trees, shares Wu. Vegetation commonly found in Southeast Asia, like bamboo and plumeria, were pushed and stretched. Fantasy creatures came next. "Kumandra is home to fantasy animals of all shapes, sizes, and colors," Briggs reports.

And then came crowds. "Crowds are challenging," admits Loftis. "They have to work cohesively as a giant group. If one thing stands out too much, the audience can get distracted by the background and lose focus on the main character and her performance." On the costume front, "the key to designing for crowds is to work smarter, not harder," advises costume designer Neysa Bové. "We looked for items like tunics that could work

many different ways—long, shorter, belted, sleeves rolled up or down. We played with different ways of draping fabrics and experimented with pectoral necklaces and chokers set symmetrically or asymmetrically and mixed with modern jewelry."

Most characters wear a version of a *sampot* pant, "a long, rectangular piece of cloth, often four meters in length, that is deftly wrapped around the waist, drawn between the legs from the front and tucked in the back," describes simulation supervisor Avneet Kaur. For Kaur, creating them in CG has been a career highlight. "The *sampot* is a remarkable garment. It's very difficult to drape in real life, forget CG. And it has no seams but when secured will stay firmly in place, regardless of whether the wearer is fighting, dancing, or going about everyday life."

Water also plays a central role in the film, both as a life-provider and as protector against the Druun. Inspired by the Mekong, the beloved "mother river" of Southeast Asia, Kumandra's Dragon River is a crucial feature of its topography and the setting for much of Raya's journey. "The Dragon River runs from Fang through Heart, Spine, and Talon and ends in Tail," details environment look supervisor Benjamin Min Huang. "To communicate where Raya is on her journey, we developed different hues for different sections of the river. The waters near Fang are fed by waterfalls. They're fresh, blue, and clear. For more stagnant water, like those around Heart, we added a green hue to represent algae. Shallow water, like in the desert of Tail where the lands are dried up, is brown and muddy."

"The world of Kumandra is a fantasy, filled with otherworldly creatures and unique environments, but underneath it all, our goal is for the audience to sense an authentic 'fragrance' of Southeast Asia," says Shurer. "I hope that when people from the region see our world," adds head of story Fawn Veerasunthorn, "they can feel the love we put into its design."

Larry Wu: Digital

HEART

THE HEART LANDS represent the spiritual center of the world once known as Kumandra. Located on a natural island, Heart, with its distinctive round rock formation, is home to the magical Dragon Gem said to protect the realm from evil forces. The people of Heart are the most prosperous of all the lands. They believe the ancient dragons entrusted the Gem to them for safekeeping, and for hundreds of years they have carefully guarded it.

"Design-wise, everything in *Raya and the Last Dragon* started with Heart," says production designer Paul Felix, who recalls feeling the pressure to "get it right" early on. "Not only would Heart set the tone for every other land," he admits, "but it would also carry tremendous storytelling significance as a representation of everything that used to be right in Kumandra and as the home to our main character, Raya." Director Don Hall elaborates: "Heart represents Raya's happy place—her father and her people."

Central to Heart's design are dragons. "In this way, Heart, of all of the five lands, is most inspired by Southeast Asia, where sacred beings are venerated through physical representations and imagery," explains production designer Mingjue Helen Chen. In Heart, dragon statues made of karst limestone protect important locations, like the sacred Heart Fortress and chiefly Heart Palace. They fortify significant structures, like the symbolic Heart Bridge. They are found in intricate sandstone carvings inside and outside of buildings and even on clothing worn by Heart people.

"Our dragon, like the *naga*, is connected to water. So too is Heart's design language, which relies heavily on water for inspiration," says Felix. Raindrops, ripples, fluid, flowing patterns, and floral motifs fill Heart, as do cool, watery blues and greens. "Everything in Heart is rounded, from the towers of its architecture to its city layout, which, from a bird's-eye view, looks like ripples," adds Chen. Even Heart's most distinctive natural landmark—a massive rock formerly known as "the Eye"—draws inspiration from a raindrop. Designed early on by Felix, it led to an important "aha!" moment for the team. "Paul's painting of Heart Temple perched on that giant rock—masterfully lit and set in a lush, wet world reminiscent of the places we visited in Laos, Indonesia, Thailand, and Vietnam—for the first time captured the visual potential of our film," says co-director Paul Briggs. "We couldn't wait for it to be realized."

Paul Felix: Digital

(previous spread) **Ryan Lang:** Digital

(next page) **Various Artists:** Digital

RIPPLES/DROPS

AQUATIC COLORS

FLORAL
MOTIFS

THE DRAGON
5 LANDS MOTIFS

FLOWING MOTIFS

CITY/VILLAGE
LAYOUT

THE HEART LANDS ARE HEAVILY TIED TO WATER. ITS RIPPLES AND FLOWING PATTERNS CAN BE FOUND EVERYWHERE IN HEART DESIGN. THE WATER DROP ITSELF IS INSPIRATION FOR THE TOWERS OF HEART. HEART COLORS MIMIC THE WATER COOL GREENS AND BLUES DOMINATE THE PALETTE.

Paul Felix: Digital

Mingjue Helen Chen: Digital

The central motif in Heart is the circle, echoing the circular ripple created by a drop of rain.
—Paul Felix, Production Designer

Mingjue Helen Chen: Digital

Mingjue Helen Chen: Digital

Paul Felix: Digital

As Benja's dream to return to a united Kumandra came into sharper focus in the story, the idea that he would have to bridge serious gaps between the disparate lands inspired us to create a literal bridge, which became the ideal backdrop for his stirring speech. —**Carlos López Estrada, Director**

Mingjue Helen Chen: Digital

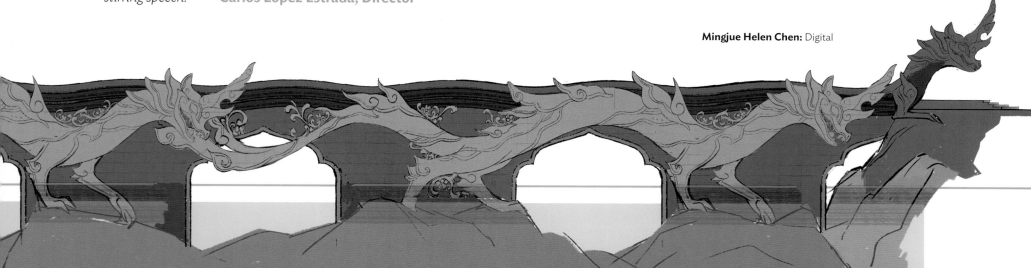

Mehrdad Isvandi: Digital

Mingjue Helen Chen: Digital

Heart Palace pushes only two colors: blue with gold accents. The amount of blue is almost overwhelming. We did that to ensure that even if we only spent a few seconds in Heart in the beginning of the film, the audience would remember "this blue location means Heart" in a flashback.
—**Mehrdad Isvandi, Visual Development Artist**

Mehrdad Isvandi: Digital

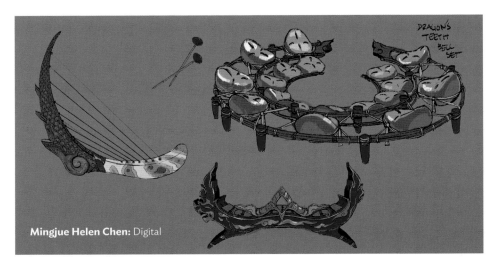

Mingjue Helen Chen: Digital

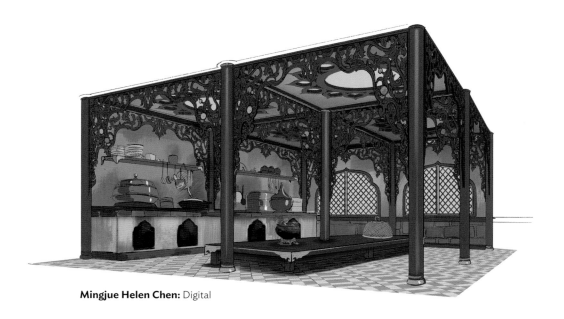

Mingjue Helen Chen: Digital

The visual development team did a fantastic job of creating a kitchen setting that reflects the communal cooking experience of Southeast Asia. The lower table at the center, where people prepare and share their meals, is an intimate and familiar place to feel the bond between a father and daughter. It was important to me that we see and hear the names of specific ingredients from the region, like shrimp paste, lemongrass, and kaffir lime leaves, and that audiences at home could use these same ingredients to make the soup Benja made for his daughter. —**Fawn Veerasunthorn, Head of Story**

April Liu: Digital

Within Heart there has always been a beautiful pond where the Dragon Gem is kept, visualized early on by production designer Paul Felix. We knew this location would be the setting of an important moment between Raya and her father, so for weeks I agonized over how to make it feel like a truly magical and sacred place. I researched flowers that only bloom at night and found an art installation involving lamps made of silk that would glow stronger and dimmer depending on how close a person was to it. This inspired the idea of flowers, eventually named the Kumandra Flower, that would light up when the Dragon Gem, a symbol of hope, was near. Thematically, it represented the idea that one light can light the world. —**John Ripa, Co-director**

Mingjue Helen Chen: Digital

Mingjue Helen Chen: Digital

71

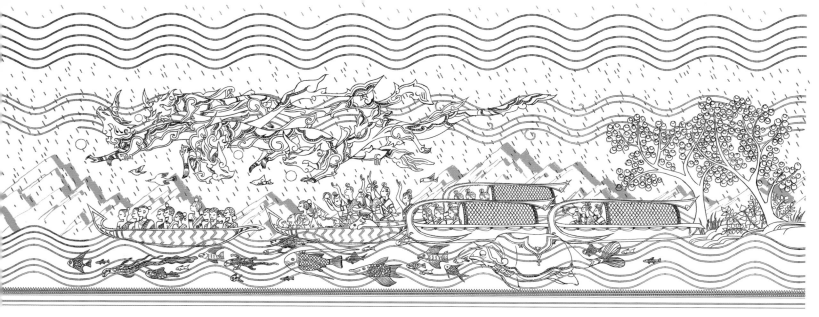

Mingjue Helen Chen: Digital

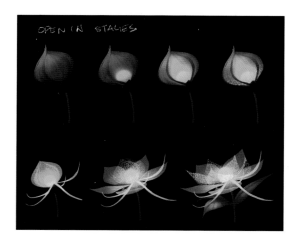

Mingjue Helen Chen: Digital

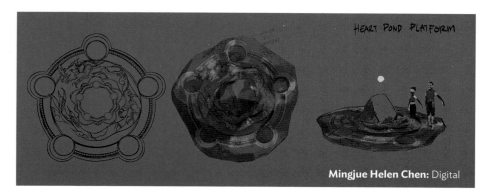

Mingjue Helen Chen: Digital

Heart Fortress was built around where Sisu left her Dragon Gem. Drawing inspiration from Angkor Wat in Cambodia, the dome-shaped Heart Fortress is incredibly detailed. Many intricate bas-relief carvings that honor the ancient dragons adorn its walls. Five dragons representing the five lands were carved into the center of the temple to encircle the Gem and protect it. Its location on the highest point of all of Heart gives it the most esteemed position in the land. —**Mingjue Helen Chen, Production Designer**

Mehrdad Isvandi: Digital

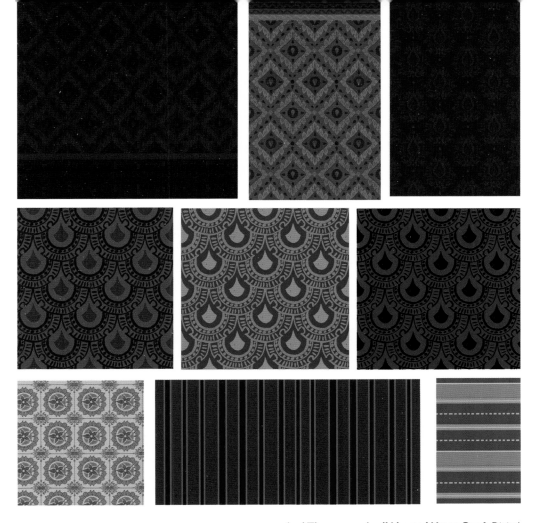

Ami Thompson, April Liu, and Neysa Bové: Digital

Ami Thompson: Digital

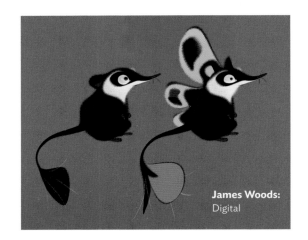

James Woods:
Digital

Early on we needed a fantasy animal for an animation test. Co-director John Ripa had this little creature in some of his storyboards, so we threw it over to James Woods in visual development to better realize it. It seemed like your run-of-the-mill shrew until a drop of water hit it and a cool aqua fin popped up! We were sold! —**Paul Briggs, Co-director**

BENJA

Chief of Heart and loving father to Raya, Benja, aka "the baddest blade in the five lands," is a noble ruler who takes his duty to protect the Dragon Gem for all very seriously. He is dignified, and has a warm, fuzzy side only Raya can see.   **—Adele Lim, Screenwriter**

Nicholas Orsi: Digital

[Smiles warmly]

Ami Thompson: Digital

Ami Thompson: Digital

Ami Thompson: Digital

I think a lot of us parents can relate to Benja. He aspires to make a better world for his daughter, greater than the one he entered into. —**Paul Briggs, Co-director**

Neysa Bové: Digital

Benja wears over his shoulder a draped brocade silk scarf ornamented with dragons riding through the clouds on raindrops, leaf and flower icons from Heart, and a trim made up of beautiful glass and gold beads. Two regal dragons facing each other form a neck piece fit for a chief. —**Neysa Bové, Costume Designer**

THE DRUUN

The Druun are indifferent, otherworldly entities that thrive on despondence and discord, and multiply through the absorption of human spirits. They are the physical embodiment of hopelessness and consume life indiscriminately. Our goal for their character design was to create a form that was ever-changing, difficult to perceive as one continuous form, and seeming to always take in, never give back, so much so that it even consumes itself. Aquatic life, water boiling in reverse, dough folding in on itself, black holes, and parasitic behaviors all fed into the structure and motion design of the Druun.

—Michael Kaschalk, Head of Effects Animation

Shiyoon Kim: Digital

Cory Loftis: Digital

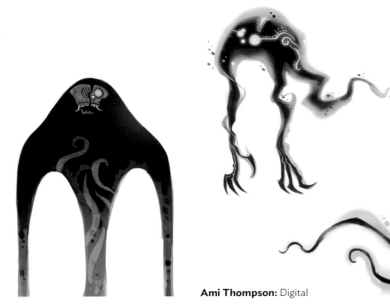

Ami Thompson: Digital

From the beginning, we had the challenge of creating the ominous character of the Druun. They had to interact with our other characters and environments and be unlike anything we'd ever seen before, all while keeping the development time and the complexity of animating the Druun to a manageable level. Our effects department rose to the occasion and created a multi-layered simulation that meets all the requirements and is terrifying on screen.
—Kyle Odermatt, VFX Supervisor

Ryan Lang: Digital

Peter DeMund: Digital

Paul Briggs: Digital

Our teams have had a lot of fun with the Druun. They're Druuntastic! We affectionately nicknamed their CG placeholder "blob," "potato sack," "kidney," "stomach," and, most commonly used, "the bladder." When a Druun splits after consuming a soul, we call the original Druun "Momma Druun" and the new one "Baby Druun."
— **Michael Kaschalk, Head of Effects Animation**

Paul Felix: Digital

TAIL

TAIL

TAIL IS THE MOST REMOTE, undeveloped land in Kumandra. It is a place for outliers, explorers, and others who have no use for structure and rules. The people of Tail used to live off the Dragon River, traveling on boats to set up homesteads in far-flung areas. But when the Dragon Gem was broken and water became more scarce, the river began to dry up, boats were grounded, and the people found themselves in a barren landscape.

Raya arrives in the Tail Lands after six hard, unsuccessful years of searching for Sisu. "Tail is the end of the road for Raya," says director Don Hall. "It's the last and final place Sisu could be. From a storytelling perspective, we loved how the harsh desert environment of Tail visually accentuates Raya's bleak circumstances."

"From the beginning, Tail has been fairly consistent design-wise," explains production designer Paul Felix. "It's the 'wild west' of our world." Early on, Felix looked to red rock canyons for inspiration and credits visual development artist Ryan Lang for "finding" Tail. "Ryan's early landscape studies became exactly what we needed. They had these really fantastic landforms that he found and exaggerated, like fantasy plateaus with sand waterfalls."

Tail's design is influenced by its desert surroundings and the improvisational approach of its denizens, who recycle everything from clothing to buildings. "Even though they are farther away from the other clans, they are still connected by the Dragon River. Remnants of a seafaring culture are abundant, so we see a lot of the scavenged boats and docks in our sets," expounds production designer Mingjue Helen Chen.

But despite its seemingly sparse landscape, "Tail is actually a pretty complex set in CG because of how close the camera needs to get to the desert floor," says head of environments Larry Wu. "Many of the cracks had to be modeled by hand. Plus, there are a lot of little elements like rocks, pebbles, and small, dried vegetation that add complexity. And to top it off, it's always sunny in Tail—so we can't hide! We had to figure out all the details."

(previous spread) **Ryan Lang:** Digital

(above) **Kevin Nelson:** Digital

(next page) **Various Artists:** Digital

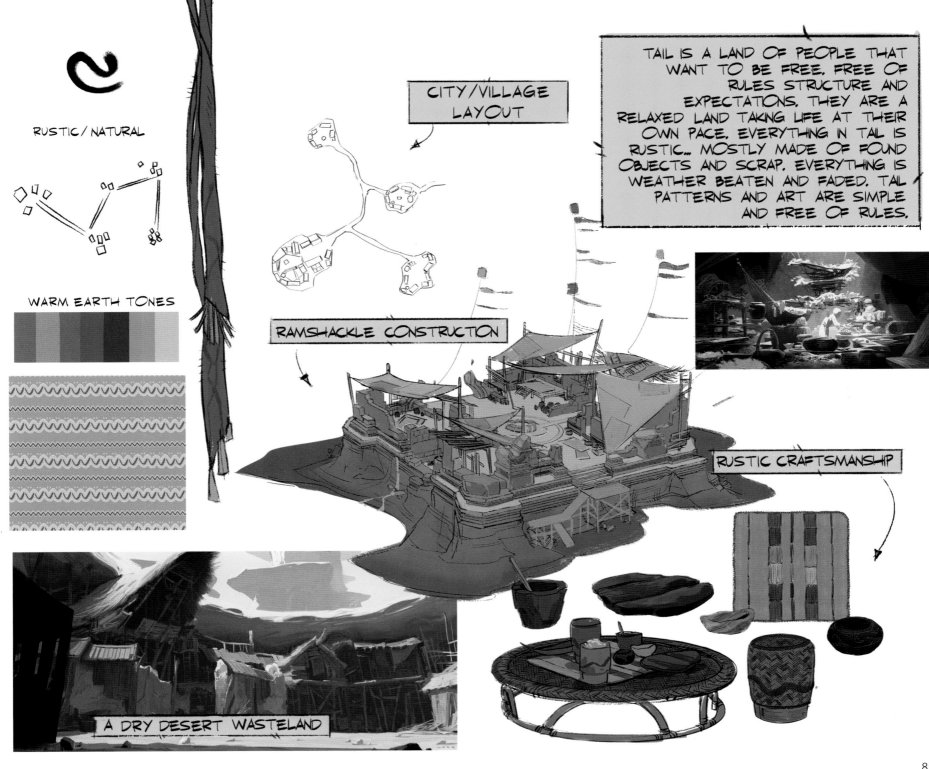

RUSTIC / NATURAL

WARM EARTH TONES

CITY/VILLAGE LAYOUT

TAIL IS A LAND OF PEOPLE THAT WANT TO BE FREE. FREE OF RULES STRUCTURE AND EXPECTATIONS. THEY ARE A RELAXED LAND TAKING LIFE AT THEIR OWN PACE. EVERYTHING IN TAIL IS RUSTIC... MOSTLY MADE OF FOUND OBJECTS AND SCRAP. EVERYTHING IS WEATHER BEATEN AND FADED. TAIL PATTERNS AND ART ARE SIMPLE AND FREE OF RULES.

RAMSHACKLE CONSTRUCTON

RUSTIC CRAFTSMANSHIP

A DRY DESERT WASTELAND

Tail nods to the Western films that inspired us in early design exploration. Back then, Raya was known as the fearsome "Dragon Blade" who traveled the lands fighting the Druun. That story idea changed over time, and the Druun became ethereal and unfightable, but Raya remained a fierce, determined warrior, and Tail maintained its vast and stark photographic aesthetic. —**Paul Felix, Production Designer**

(this page) **Ryan Lang:** Digital

Kevin Nelson: Digital

Raya escapes the Druun by being thrown into the Dragon River by her father in Heart, and we cut immediately to six years later, in the arid desert of Tail. The contrast between the two environments—cool, blue water to warm, hot, dry desert—is extremely stark. To amplify the arid feeling of a desert, we are playing with light distortion to create a kind of mirage, a rippling you would see in a dry, hot place. By pairing a dramatic shift in lighting, color, climate, and water with the inciting incident of the film, we hope to visually express the feeling of the "drop" that our main character experiences.
—**Adolph Lusinsky, Director of Cinematography-Lighting**

Mingjue Helen Chen: Digital

Mehrdad Isvandi: Digital

Mehrdad Isvandi: Digital

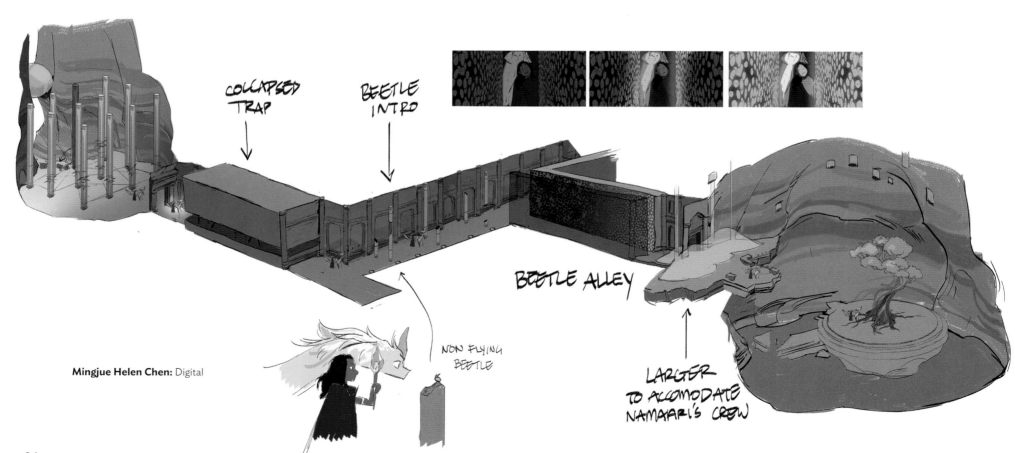

COLLAPSED TRAP

BEETLE INTRO

BEETLE ALLEY

Mingjue Helen Chen: Digital

NON FLYING BEETLE

LARGER TO ACCOMODATE NAMAARI'S CREW

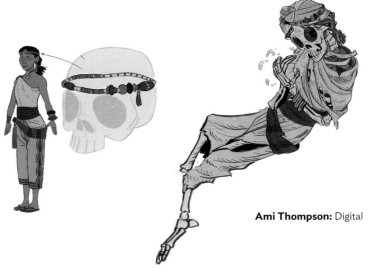

Ami Thompson: Digital

We're always trying to find visual ways to express metaphors for the lands themselves. In Tail, people are long—they're "tail-like." Visual development artist Kevin Nelson, who designed Tail Dock, included these flying kites with really long tails. Tail banners, too, are very long. They clearly say "Tail!"
—**Mingjue Helen Chen, Production Designer**

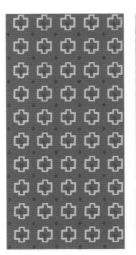

Ami Thompson: Digital

Ami Thompson: Digital

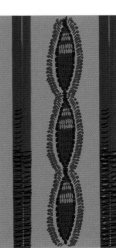

Ami Thompson and Paul Felix: Digital

BOUN

Boun is a precocious street kid from Tail. He's an adult in a child's body, capable and self-sufficient. He is the self-styled owner, manager, chef, and captain of his own shrimp boat. Deep down, he's a vulnerable child who lost his parents to the Druun.
—**Dean Wellins, Director, Pre-production**

Shiyoon Kim: Digital

James Woods: Digital

Shiyoon Kim: Digital

Boun was designed to give the feeling of a cute, fuzzy, little mouse. He's very small in stature. He smiles open-mouthed with all of his teeth that are in a bit of an overbite and chipped. His thick, tousled head of hair makes you just want to reach out and scruff it up.
—**Shiyoon Kim, Art Director of Characters**

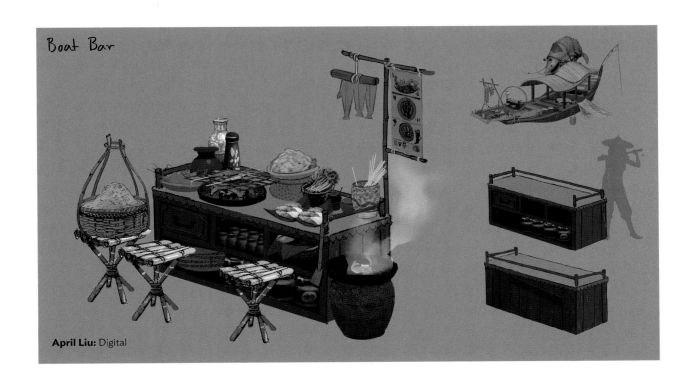

Boat Bar

April Liu: Digital

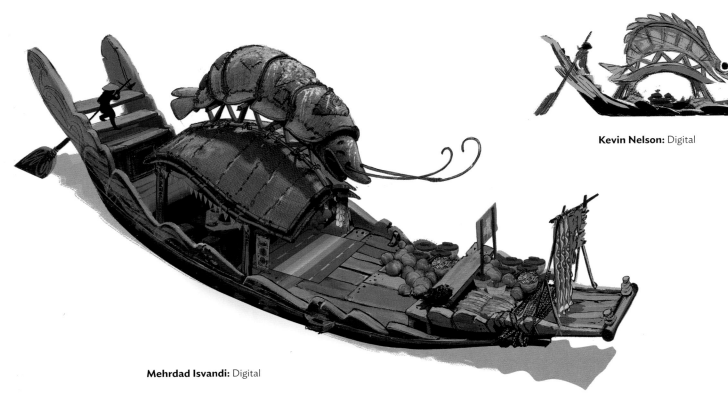

Mehrdad Isvandi: Digital

Kevin Nelson: Digital

Boun was always a little businessman but changed land of origin a few times. He started off as a mechanic from Tail who Raya hired to fix one of Tuk Tuk's "tires" when a Druun arm got stuck in it, then became a hustler of knickknacks in Talon, and then returned to Tail selling shrimp rice soup on his shrimp boat. —**John Ripa, Co-director**

TALON

TALON

THE TALON LANDS are the trading crossroads of the five lands, a melting pot filled with worldly travelers and merchants. Its vibrant, bustling market port, set on the Dragon River, is crammed with vendors in fantastical boats and bright storefronts vying for business. Talon's design revolves around its merchants, who are the lifeblood of its economy. For the merchants, portability is important, as are the bright colors and patterns they use to draw attention to their merchandise.

"Every epic fantasy film needs a watering hole, and Talon is ours," reveals co-director Paul Briggs. "Like the cantina in *Star Wars*, Talon is a place where people from all walks of life converge, selling things, bartering, and trading—a pure pop of color and fantasy."

Southeast Asia's famous water markets on the Mekong River in Vietnam and the night markets of Thailand and Laos provided inspiration for the floating city's look and feel. For screenwriter Adele Lim, Talon really captures the feeling of the region. "There," she says, "the day-to-day is filled with hustle and bustle. Everyone is all up in each other's business. It's hectic and sometimes messy and super chaotic. But everyone has a purpose, and everyone is in it together." Adds director Carlos López Estrada: "Talon feels so alive. It's bright, colorful, and chaotic, an exciting collision of stimuli."

Visual development artist Kevin Nelson first explored Talon by building a pier that had not one, but five different levels. "Kevin's wild multilevel set, with its amazing catwalks going across, in, and out, brought Talon's design language to new heights, literally," laughs director, pre-production Dean Wellins. For Nelson, function drove fantasy. "We knew Talon was in a drought for story reasons, so my thinking was to start at the top level where the waterline had been years before. Then, as the waterline lowered, new platforms would've been built underneath so people could access their boats." Production designer Paul Felix credits Nelson's roofs—thatched from recycled boat sails, fabrics, grasses, and palm fronds—for establishing the unique patchwork quality of Talon's aesthetic.

Seafood also provided inspiration for the shape language of Talon. Says head of environments Larry Wu, "Talon is full of fish. Fresh and dried fish hang all over the market to be sold, and giant fantasy fish swim in the river. The rooflines of Talon take on a fish-like shape. We even have boats shaped like fish, crabs, squid, and turtles."

Unsurprisingly, the busy set of Talon is also the film's most complex. "It's our environment with the most elements, assets, models, and characters, and they all need to move around on the water," says environment model supervisor Eric Provan. Wu adds that the handmade quality of the set, including "patterns and weaves in different bamboo and straw, rope-tied huts made of bamboo and wood, and intricately hand-sewn textiles lining the walls," only increases its complexity. "Our teams had our work cut out for us with Talon," he laughs.

Mingjue Helen Chen: Digital

(previous spread) **Kevin Nelson:** Digital

(next page) **Various Artists:** Digital

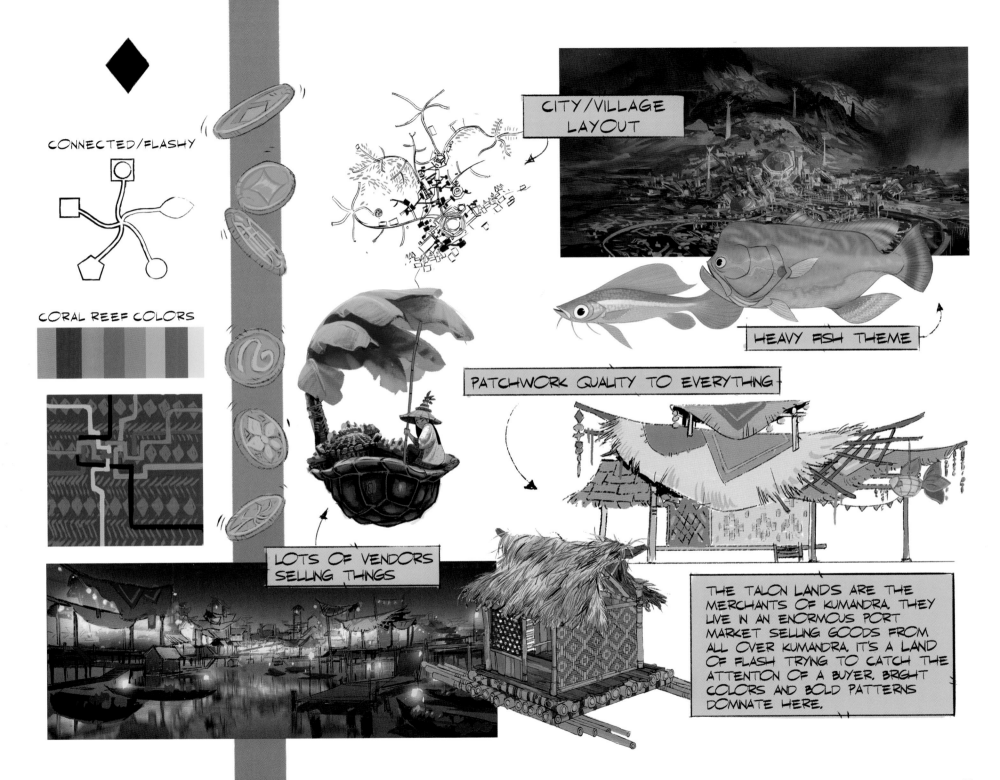

CONNECTED/FLASHY

CORAL REEF COLORS

CITY/VILLAGE LAYOUT

HEAVY FISH THEME

PATCHWORK QUALITY TO EVERYTHING

LOTS OF VENDORS SELLING THINGS

THE TALON LANDS ARE THE MERCHANTS OF KUMANDRA. THEY LIVE IN AN ENORMOUS PORT MARKET SELLING GOODS FROM ALL OVER KUMANDRA. IT'S A LAND OF FLASH TRYING TO CATCH THE ATTENTION OF A BUYER. BRIGHT COLORS AND BOLD PATTERNS DOMINATE HERE.

Kevin Nelson: Digital

Design-wise, Talon keeps things simple in a very busy way. Each individual structure is loud and loaded with stuff. But when you really look, they appear to be grouped together to form only a very few shapes.
—**Kevin Nelson, Visual Development Artist**

April Liu: Digital

April Liu: Digital

Kevin Nelson: Digital

April Liu: Digital

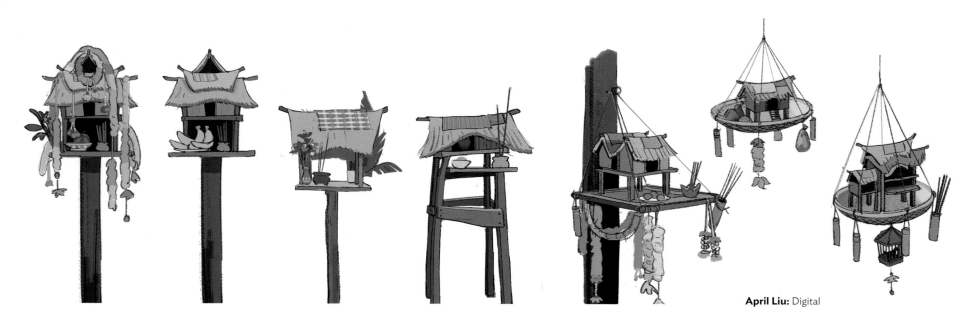

April Liu: Digital

Mehrdad Isvandi: Digital

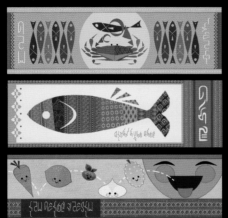

Brittney Lee: Digital

Talon boats started off as rounded tugboats. Then we pushed ourselves to design something you could never actually find in a book about boats. Given that Talon traders are resourceful and always competing for a buyer's attention, we wondered: What if one trader turned a giant turtle shell he found into a cool boat? And then maybe that turtle shell boat inspired another trader to make a boat shaped like a giant shrimp, cuttlefish, or horseshoe crab. —**Mehrdad Isvandi, Visual Development Artist**

Talon needed to feel as lively as a real market, so we designed all these merchant stalls and filled them with baskets of fresh produce and fish, steaming foods for sale, and other fantastical items. Then, we lit them with multicolored lanterns in various geometric and organic shapes. The stalls are also set-dressed with spirit houses. Found throughout Southeast Asia, the tiny houses are miniature shrines placed outside homes and businesses and adorned with offerings such as fruits, flowers, and incense in the hope that spirits will congregate there and provide good luck.
—**April Liu, Visual Development Artist**

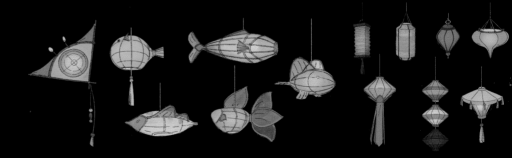

April Liu: Digital

The shape of Talon chief Dang Hai's home was inspired by an angler fish. Giant poles protruding out of the stilt house nod to the many kinds of poles used on the Mekong—fishing poles, flag poles, and bamboo push poles that are used to move boats. On the poles hang glass lanterns. We painted a texture on the roof to give the appearance of a curved, multilayered patchwork of thatch.
—**James Finch, Visual Development Artist**

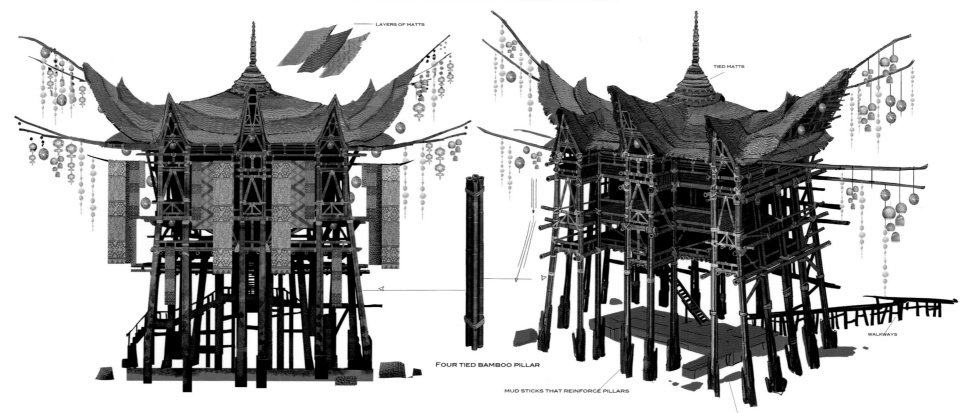

LAYERS OF MATTS

TIED MATTS

FOUR TIED BAMBOO PILLAR

MUD STICKS THAT REINFORCE PILLARS

WALKWAYS

ROCK PLATFORM REMNANTS

(this page) **James Finch:** Digital

Ami Thompson: Digital

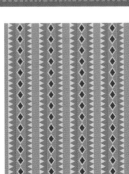

Chief Dang Hai of Talon and his mother, Dang Hu, may secretly be my favorite of the Lands' chiefs. Dang Hai just tickled our imagination. Dang Hu is very much inspired by my own immigrant grandmother. On the outside, she looks so small and sweet. But scratch the surface, she's all fire—a strong personality who isn't intimidated by anybody, a true Vietnamese matriarch.
—Qui Nguyen, Screenwriter

Ami Thompson and April Liu: Digital

THE ONGIS

The three Ongis are part-monkey, part-catfish mochi balls with fur. We designed them to look super cute and approachable. They're round, soft, and fluffy. You just want to squeeze them! They also have long, catfish whiskers and fins for ears and tails. Each has a different personality: One is friendly, one is serious, and the other is derpy.
—**Ami Thompson, Art Director of Characters**

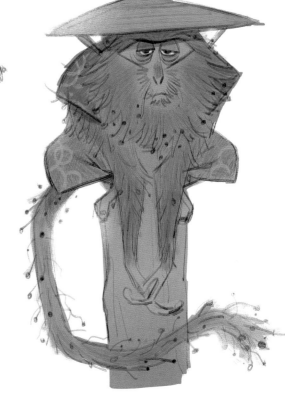

Shiyoon Kim: Digital

Scott Watanabe: Digital

Shiyoon Kim: Digital

Griselda Sastrawinata: Digital

100

(this page) **Ami Thompson:** Digital

The Ongis posed a few fun challenges for our rigging team. First of all, they had to be very squishy with extremely pliable bodies. Their whiskers had to clear their large, expressive mouths. And the Ongis are both bipeds and quadrupeds. They needed to sprint, jump, swim, and fight interchangeably between two and four legs. —**Walt Yoder, Character Rigging Supervisor**

LITTLE NOI

Little Noi is a business baby. She doesn't give in easily to charm, and you have to work hard for her respect. When we paired Noi with the Ongis, we needed to get the sense that she's safe, she's not in danger, and she's not sad being abandoned. Her toughness gives us a sense of ease. Even though the Ongis are maternal to her, she gives the impression that she's actually the boss running the whole operation.
—**Fawn Veerasunthorn, Head of Story**

(this page) **Ami Thompson:** Digital

(this page) **Cory Loftis:** Digital

SPINE

KUMANDRA'S FIERCEST WARRIORS call the spectacular, snowy, giant black bamboo mountains of the Spine Lands home. Defensive and protective of their settlements, the people of Spine are known for being ferociously unwelcoming to strangers. Over the years they have adapted to their preference for isolation and insularity by becoming completely self-sufficient, living off only what they can find and grow in their extreme mountainous environment, which is mostly bamboo. "A Spine warrior eats, wears, wields, and lives in bamboo," says co-director John Ripa. But not just any bamboo, production designer Paul Felix explains. "In Spine, bamboo grows as big as redwood trees."

Inspired by their mega surroundings, the people of Spine design with a "large and chunky aesthetic," notes production designer Mingjue Helen Chen. "Playing with scale also helped us push the fantastical feeling of the mountainside," adds Felix. His early pass of the Spine village meeting hall, which included a giant black bamboo frame and a colossal woolly mammoth–like tusked roofline constructed from individual pieces of bamboo tied together, gave the team a benchmark for Spine's structural design approach. "Spine design also leans into natural forms and textures," says visual development artist James Finch. "We thought, for example, that they might lift their structures off the snow line by placing them on carefully constructed large stone foundations sourced from the surrounding rocky mountain."

Cinematographically, Spine's stark color palette—"white snow, black bamboo that becomes a deep blue when lit, with hints of maroon leaves," as Chen describes it—heightens the epic feel of Spine. "Our early explorations of Spine incorporated a lost-and-found approach to edges, which really packed a punch given how dramatic Spine bamboo and structures are," shares Felix. "When Raya and the crew arrive in Spine, we will sense they are coming up to a settlement, but we don't see all the details of that settlement. It's just amassing."

Cory Loftis: Digital

(previous spread) **Paul Felix:** Digital

(next page) **Various Artists:** Digital

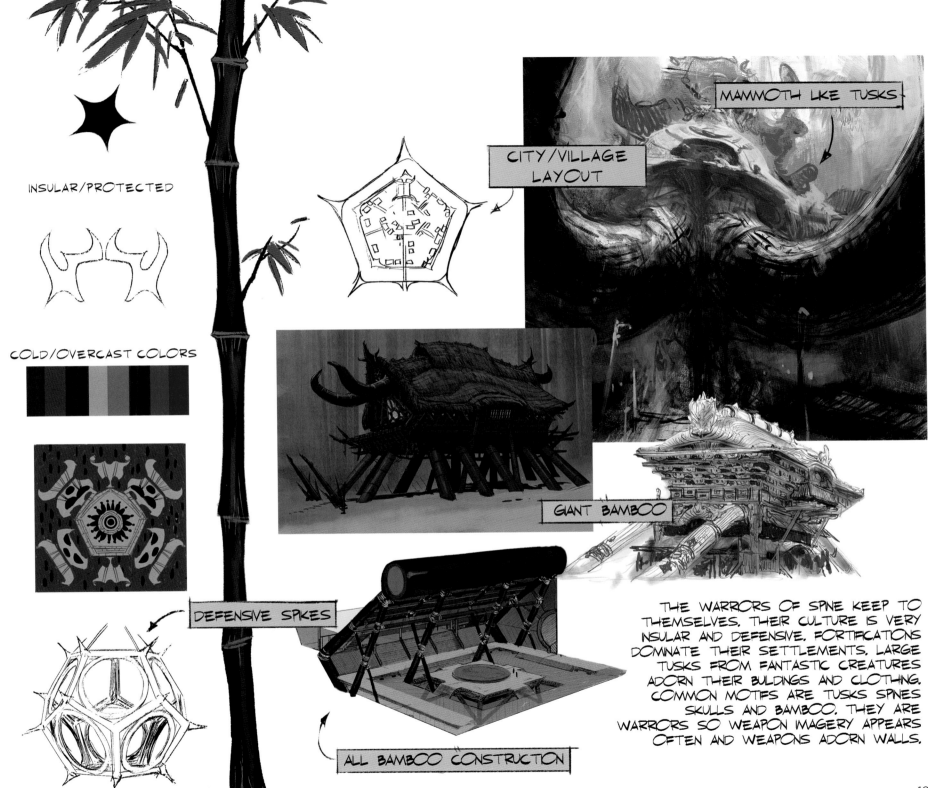

INSULAR/PROTECTED

COLD/OVERCAST COLORS

DEFENSIVE SPIKES

CITY/VILLAGE LAYOUT

MAMMOTH LIKE TUSKS

GIANT BAMBOO

ALL BAMBOO CONSTRUCTION

THE WARRIORS OF SPINE KEEP TO THEMSELVES. THEIR CULTURE IS VERY INSULAR AND DEFENSIVE. FORTIFICATIONS DOMINATE THEIR SETTLEMENTS. LARGE TUSKS FROM FANTASTIC CREATURES ADORN THEIR BUILDINGS AND CLOTHING. COMMON MOTIFS ARE TUSKS SPINES SKULLS AND BAMBOO. THEY ARE WARRIORS SO WEAPON IMAGERY APPEARS OFTEN AND WEAPONS ADORN WALLS.

Mingjue Helen Chen: Digital

Mingjue Helen Chen: Digital

The scenes outside the Spine gates are some of my favorites. The stark beauty of the white snow against the blue-black of the giant bamboo, framed by maroon leaves, creates a perfect setting for some incredible fight scenes.
—**Osnat Shurer, Producer**

Mingjue Helen Chen: Digital

James Finch: Digital

Mingjue Helen Chen: Digital

Mingjue Helen Chen: Digital

Spine Temple is so unique. The sacred structure needed to be the most impressive, and in a forest of giant bamboo, what could be more impressive than the biggest one of them all?
—**Mingjue Helen Chen, Production Designer**

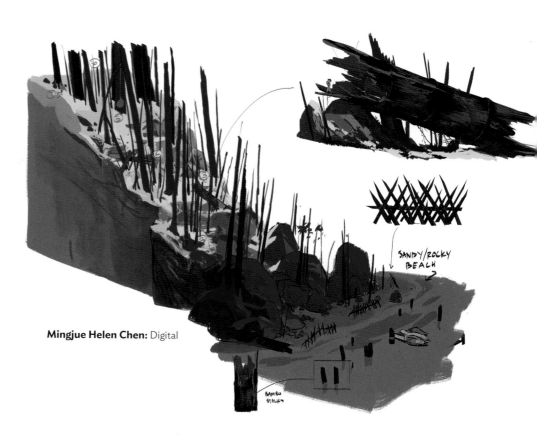

Mingjue Helen Chen: Digital

James Finch: Digital

Base is Large Bamboo spokes

April Liu: Digital

James Finch:
Digital

Spine's climate is cold and snowy, unlike much of Southeast Asia. We tried to keep the multi-windowed high rooftops of structures you might find in Laos and Indonesia but thought that instead of ventilation for the heat, the rooftops could ventilate smoke from a fire. The roofs, made from thick, thatched woven straw, give the feeling of "mammoth warm."
—James Finch, Visual Development Artist

Where I grew up in the Philippines, most homes are decorated with a large wooden spoon and fork, a cultural staple that represents health and prosperity. Families invite friends and neighbors to all come together and share fellowship over a nice, warm meal. —**Virgilio John Aquino, Environment Modeler**

James Finch: Digital

Mingjue Helen Chen: Digital

Mingjue Helen Chen: Digital

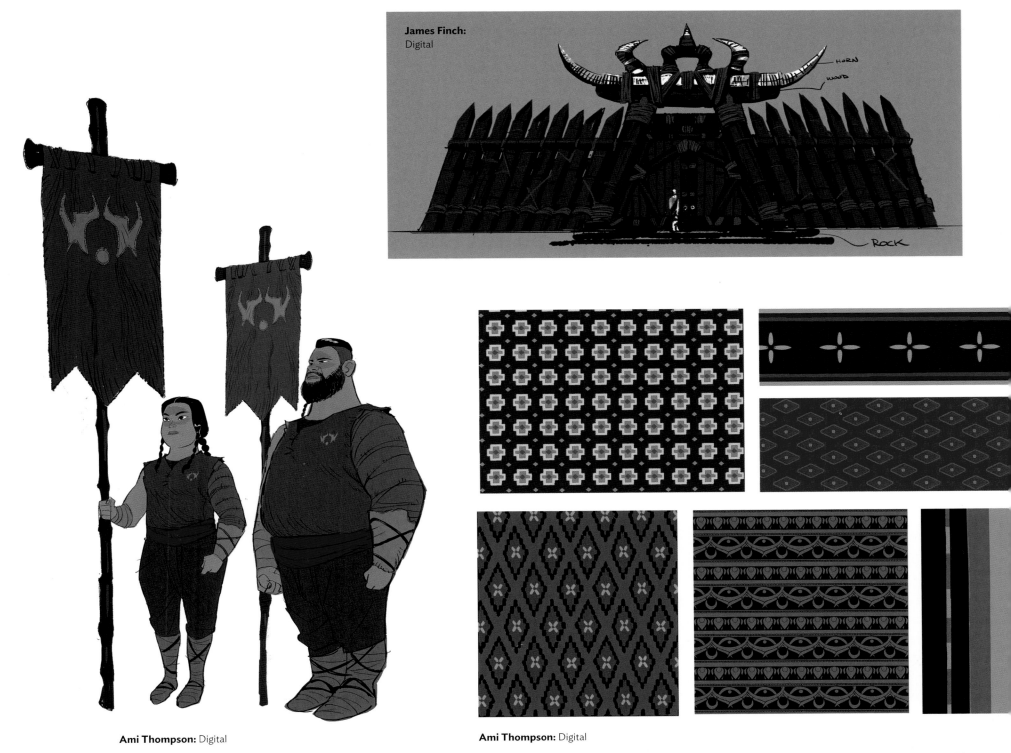

James Finch: Digital

HORN

WOOD

ROCK

Ami Thompson: Digital

Ami Thompson: Digital

113

TONG

(this page) **Ami Thompson:** Digital

Huge, grizzled, super-fierce, and wielding a giant battle axe, Tong is the quintessential Spine warrior. However, beneath that rough exterior lies the soul of an offbeat poet whose heart melts when he meets Little Noi.
—**Don Hall, Director**

Like his size, Tong's model from a CG complexity perspective is pretty impressive. Up top he wears six different pelts that are quilted onto him and on bottom a traditional wrapped sampot pant. He's got armor, wraps, food items hanging from his belt, and an eye patch. Performance-wise, not only is he a seasoned warrior who would need to be in the middle of all the action, but also he is a climbing wall for Noi and the Ongis.
— **Carlos Cabral, Head of Characters and Technical Animation**

Ami Thompson: Digital

Cory Loftis and Jim Finn: Digital

FANG

FANG

FANG IS ALL ABOUT POWER. Its inhabitants resent Heart for having the Dragon Gem, which they believe brings magical prosperity, and they attempt to take it for themselves. But the Dragon Gem is shattered, and the Druun return. To protect themselves, the people of Fang dig a canal around their land. Situated near the head of the Dragon River, they are surrounded by water and become the only land that continues to thrive. "The people of Fang were originally conceived as villains," reveals director Carlos López Estrada. "But as the story continued to develop, it became clear that they, like the people from the other lands, were simply doing their best to survive."

Fang's design aesthetic mirrors its belief system. "The people are strict and stringent," says production designer Mingjue Helen Chen. The team looked to brutalism and its strong, monolithic, and rigid geometric shapes for inspiration. "Fang's large, symmetrical shapes and straight angles reinforce them as a rigid people," Chen explains. Their power color palette leans into stark white and black with red accents, and their structures are made from slick, luxurious marble and limestone.

Fang's design is also extremely vertical. Visual development artist Kevin Nelson explored stretching Fang buildings and adding a repetition of rooflines to give the ominous feeling of a large creature looking down. "Think Nostradamus or Dracula," he ruminates. "Fang is now prosperous, and its people are not at war, but there is something about its design that should give you the impression that the people are not very nice." Verticality is also reinforced inside Fang's interiors, like in Fang Palace, where tall, vertical banners and giant gold fang-like sculptures hang ominously from sky-high ceilings.

All these elements were designed to contrast with Heart. "Heart is full of floral motifs and round, organic shapes," says Chen. "We wanted to represent Fang as the opposite, so where there are shapes, they are rectangular with sharp edges. Fang decorations, unlike Heart, are sparse to give a cold, sterile feel." Adds head of environments Larry Wu, "Fang, above all, is all about precision and craftsmanship. Everything is well built and meticulously maintained."

(previous spread) **Kevin Nelson:** Digital

Paul Felix: Digital

(next page) **Various Artists:** Digital

GEOMETRIC/MAZE

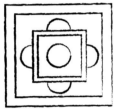

POWER COLORS

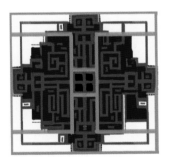

EVERYTHING IS GEOMETRIC

CITY/VILLAGE LAYOUT

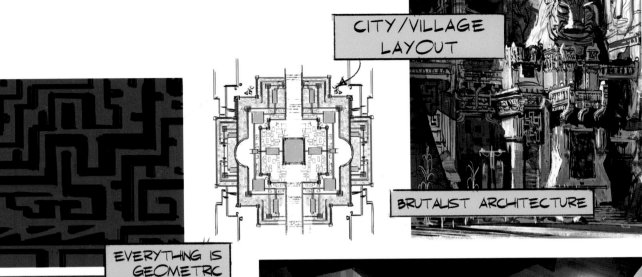

BRUTALIST ARCHITECTURE

SYMMETRY

FEROCITY

FANG IS A BRUTAL LAND THAT BELIEVES IN THE PHRASE "MIGHT IS RIGHT". POWER IS EVERYTHING IN FANG AND THEIR COLOR MOTIF IS EXCLUSIVELY POWER COLORS. STRONG GEOMETRIC SHAPES REPRESENT MAZES THAT HIGHLIGHT THE INTELLECT OF FANG PEOPLE. SECONDARY SYMBOLISM INCLUDES SHAPES THAT ARE BY THE FANGS OF THE DRAGON.

Mehrdad Isvandi: Digital

Mingjue Helen Chen: Digital

Fang went through many redesigns, but we always tried to capture the shape of fangs in its aesthetic. At first, we thought of creating high, fang-like mountains, but that was too literal. So then I thought, "What if we inverted mountain shapes, as if they've mined giant holes into the ground that could feel like tooth imprints into the land?" We had fun playing with these deep underground shapes that gave the feeling of being bitten. — **Mingjue Helen Chen, Production Designer**

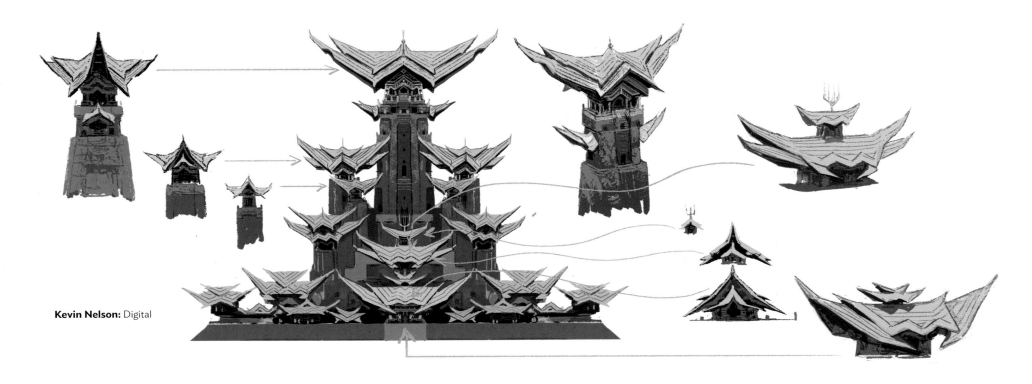

Kevin Nelson: Digital

David Womersley: Digital

Fang rooflines look like a rocket taking off. At the base, everything is wide, slow, and moving outward. Midway up, there's a feeling of acceleration and then a giant stretch to the top.
—**Kevin Nelson, Visual Development Artist**

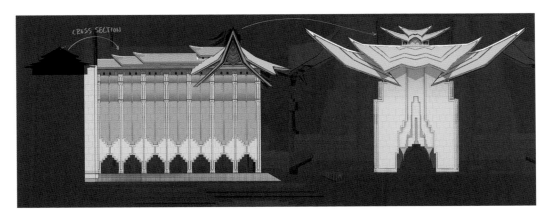

Mingjue Helen Chen: Digital

We are playing with the symmetry of Fang in layout by shooting scenes there straight on to give the feeling of reverence for royalty that is key to Fang's personality and sets it apart from every other land in our world. —**Rob Dressel, Head of Cinematography–Layout**

(this page) **Mingjue Helen Chen:** Digital

Paul Felix: Digital

I remember feeling Raya's rage in this scene the first time I heard it pitched in the story room. Raya loses herself during this fight, so we kept the timing quick and the sounds fast and sharp, so that we feel the chaos and get lost with her. Then, when she and the team face their most difficult dilemma, everything slows down and grows quiet, the sound effects drop out, and only the beautiful musical score plays, carrying the emotion. —**Shannon Stein, Editor**

April Liu: Digital

Paul Felix: Digital

Fang used to be located on the peninsula, but the inhabitants moved themselves to a small island of their own creation where they would be safer from the Druun, who cannot travel on water. The graveyard of overgrown villages and unattended rice paddies that dot the land where they used to live give you a sense of history and of their personality as a fortified people who will go to any length to protect themselves.
—**Larry Wu, Head of Environments**

April Liu: Digital

Ami Thompson: Digital

April Liu: Digital

Ami Thompson: Digital

Ami Thompson and April Liu: Digital

Same rails and base

NAMAARI

A BRILLIANT AND CALCULATING young woman, Namaari is in every way Raya's enemy. As girls, Namaari and Raya bonded over their love of dragons. But when Namaari deceived Raya to help her people steal the coveted Dragon Gem from Heart, things became personal between the two. Wherever Raya goes, Namaari is right on her heels, chasing her down.

"On the outside, Namaari is very severe, but behind the facade is a leader who feels a great responsibility to care for her people," says director Don Hall. For Namaari, the pressure for her to grow up started very young. "She was raised by a hard mother, the powerful Chief Virana of Fang, who drove her as a child," says screenwriter Adele Lim. "She is a sincere dragon nerd," adds Hall, "but she had to suppress her love of dragons to keep Fang safe and please her mother."

To express Namaari's strength and power, art director of characters Ami Thompson focused on her facial expressions and physicality. "Namaari is aggressive and has a super fierce stare, like a cat or a tiger. Her eyebrows are very expressive, and she even used to have fangs when she bared her teeth. I kept her body muscular to signal that she's a good, trained fighter."

"Production designer Cory Loftis first described Namaari as tough at her core," offers costume designer Neysa Bové, "so I was interested in creating an outfit for her with a really hard edge, something that said, 'Don't mess with me.'" Bové and Loftis chose a predominantly off-white color palette and referenced the geometric shapes of Fang for silhouette and patterning. "Just in case she didn't look strong and powerful enough, we added geometric shapes to her half-shaved hair," laughs Bové. "Namaari is so cool," adds Loftis. "She's got a cool costume, a cool weapon, a cool haircut, cool animal companions, and a cool backstory. The only real danger with a character like her is to not make her so cool that she steals the whole show."

Ryan Lang: Digital

Ami Thompson: Digital

Ami Thompson and Cory Loftis:
Digital

Ami Thompson: Digital

Shiyoon Kim: Digital

**Ami Thompson and
Cory Loftis:** Digital

*Everywhere Raya goes, Namaari follows: watching,
tracking, hunting. She's dangerous.*
—**Ami Thompson, Art Director of Characters**

Shiyoon Kim: Digital

127

As a child, Namaari lost to Raya in a fight. By the time Namaari meets Raya again, she's spent years perfecting her musculature and fighting techniques. She can take a hit and keep going. She's basically pure muscle. Her hand-to-hand fighting style is inspired by Muay Thai and Vovinam from Vietnam, and her weapons style is inspired by Krabi Krabong from Thailand. —**Qui Nguyen, Screenwriter**

Ami Thompson: Digital

Ami Thompson: Digital

Neysa Bové: Digital

Cory Loftis and Ami Thompson: Digital

Mingjue Helen Chen: Digital

Namaari is controlled, upright, and elegant as much as she is menacing and explosive. I love that we don't play those things as conflict: She is equally the poised, clever princess of Fang, and one of their greatest warriors. Instead, Namaari struggles with balancing the needs of the Fang people, her love and respect for dragons, and doing the right thing.
—**Justin Sklar, Animation Supervisor**

Kevin Nelson: Digital

Ami Thompson: Digital

YOUNG NAMAARI

Nicholas Orsi: Digital

Young Namaari is a kitten who acts like a tiger. I aimed to add some kind of insignia on her clothes that symbolize the Fang lands. If you look closely, you might see the same insignia pop up elsewhere!
—**Ami Thompson, Art Director of Characters**

(previous spread) **Various Artists:** CG Render

Cory Loftis: Digital

Young Namaari's costume separates her from Young Raya. Whereas Raya's is draped, soft, and blue with an overall serene feel, Namaari's is a stark white and gold that feels harsh. Even her accessories—gold cuffs with little spikes on them—are hard. She also used to have a gold wire cube that contained her hair bun. To me, that felt very much like the people of Fang: living life in a structured box but extremely tough. —Neysa Bové, Costume Designer

Neysa Bové: Digital

Mingjue Helen Chen: Digital

VIRANA

The cool and calculating chief of the Fang Lands, and mother to Raya's nemesis, Namaari, Virana leads her people with fierce pragmatism. A strong, brilliant, and unsentimental leader, she believes that decisive, ruthless action is the only way to guarantee her people's survival. —**Don Hall, Director**

(this page) **Ami Thompson:** Digital

SERLOTS

Namaari has a clowder of Serlot cats. Large, ferocious, rideable, and superfast, they work and attack on command. For their design, I referenced the serval and the caracal, which has long tufted ears and long canine teeth with distinctive black facial markings. They're from Fang, so they had to have a pair of fangs. We gave them two pairs, one that extends up and out of their mouths and another that extends down.
—**Ami Thompson, Art Director of Characters**

Cory Loftis: Digital

Ami Thompson: Digital

PART 3
WE ARE KUMANDRA

"THERE'S A MOMENT IN EVERY FILM THAT I LOVE," muses producer Osnat Shurer. "It's when all of the discussions, designs, and ideas come together, and when the characters themselves tell us who they need to be." For the team behind *Raya and the Last Dragon*, one of those magical moments materialized when Raya, Sisu, Boun, Noi, the Ongis, and Tong were finally visualized as one. "Seeing our crew in stunning concept paintings by our artists confirmed for us that all of these characters belong together," she remembers.

Director Don Hall explains. "Each character has so much personality: Sisu is our funny, hopeful, and unspeakably beautiful water dragon. Boun is a precocious ten-year-old with killer swagger. Noi is an adorable toddler con artist with her three resourceful Ongi caretakers. Finally, Tong is a giant softhearted one-eyed warrior. Once our characters could hold their own in the story, with a clear and essential part to play, we started to explore their relationships more in depth."

Screenwriter Adele Lim got a kick out of writing for what she affectionately calls the film's entertaining motley crew. "Originally our story focused on Raya as very self-driven, but over time we discovered that a richer, more appealing story could be told with the whole group." For Lim, shifting to an ensemble cast was also fortuitous. "The timber of Southeast Asia is community: When we pull together, we can affect miraculous, amazing, and transformative change. I love how Raya learns this through her relationships with the other characters."

Art director of characters Ami Thompson enjoyed designing a cast with distinctive body shapes that could fit together like a puzzle. "The Ongis are round, Tong is square, and Sisu is long and wavy. Only when our characters come together do they look complete." Adds head of characters and technical animation Carlos Cabral, "The challenge to translate their unique body shapes and movement styles into CG was beyond anything we had ever attempted before. I love the way Raya and her crew look."

The ensemble cast offered the animation team a prime opportunity to play with different personalities and levels of caricature, explains head of animation Amy Smeed. One of her favorite group moments is from a scene where Boun and Sisu describe their wildly different proposals to engage their adversary, Namaari. "Boyish Boun proposes a plan full of action. Trusting optimist Sisu suggests they give Namaari a gift. We stylized the movement in each vision to reflect the character, so Boun's is a rip-roaring adventure whereas Sisu's is all 'best friends forever!'"

Head of animation Malcon Pierce adds that the pairing of characters with contrasting personalities also made for deeper, more expressive scenes. "For example, when playing Raya as focused and poised, we could play Sisu as distracted and excited. Namaari's fierce determination, too, always paired well with Raya's witty humor. These kinds of contrasts made performances stronger, richer, and more fun to watch."

"This film, at its heart, is about coming together," reflects visual effects supervisor Kyle Odermatt, "and this has been a theme in the making of the film as well. Everyone from every department came together, despite having to work separately from our individual homes, to create every single frame."

Technical supervisor Kelsey Hurley connects the film's theme of community with the technology behind the film. "Each of our recent films has seen specific technical breakthroughs to achieve the final look: the camera and render improvements on *Big Hero 6*, the water in *Moana*, the complex environments of *Ralph Breaks the Internet*, and the volumetrics in *Frozen 2*. *Raya and the Last Dragon* brings all of these innovations together to produce visuals that have been ten plus years in the making."

"Fundamentally, *Raya and the Last Dragon* is a film about the power of unity," discloses director Carlos López Estrada. "It's a story about a group of individuals from very different backgrounds and ideologies who learn that working together will allow them to accomplish something much greater than they ever could on their own. And that is exactly what our crew did."

We speak a lot about magic in our film, but the real magic I got to witness every day was seeing our amazing story artists transform my words from fun ideas into reality. The trust we had in each other was more than just a theme in our movie; it was our story's beating heart.
—**Qui Nguyen, Screenwriter**

(previous spread) **Ami Thompson:** Digital

Clio Chiang: Digital

Allen Ostergar: Digital

Joe Mateo: Digital

Nicole Mitchell: Digital

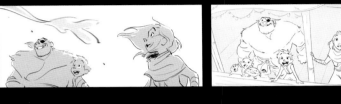

Luis Logam: Digital

Javier Ledesma Barbolla: Digital

Tom Owens: Digital

Kendelle Hoyer: Digital

Nicole Mitchell and Tom Owens: Digital

David Derrick: Digital

Sylvia Lee: Digital

Luis Logam: Digital

Donna Lee: Digital

In Southeast Asia we love to come together around food, and we realized that in the movie, food is a perfect way to visually track the arc of Raya's trust throughout her journey. As a girl, she shared meals with her beloved father, but she has been alone for many years. Now, as she finds a new family, she learns to eat with other people, and even adds to the shared food, becoming part of the community.
—**Fawn Veerasunthorn, Head of Story**

April Liu: Digital

I like to think of our characters as a mixed bag of candies. Although each has a different personality, they come together to make a happy band of buddies. To me, these characters symbolize the harmony and peace that come from groups of people overcoming their differences together. —**Ami Thompson, Art Director of Characters**

CINEMATOGRAPHY

Driven by story, the cinematography of Raya and the Last Dragon is designed to emphasize Raya's character arc and her distrust of the world outside her own. We wanted trust and distrust to drive our camera and lighting choices, so we set up guidelines based on these themes.

To illustrate the difference between trust and distrust, we chose camera and lighting styles that would contrast with each other. This visual contrast could then be applied sequence to sequence, or even shot to shot, depending on where we were in Raya's story arc.

For example, in these film frames, Raya and Sisu are engaged in a disagreement about whether or not they should trust others on their journey. Distrustful Raya was shot with a wide lens, deep focus, and a narrow color palette, while trusting Sisu was shot with a long lens, shallow focus, and a broader color palette.

—Adolph Lusinsky, Director of Cinematography-Lighting, and Rob Dressel, Director of Cinematography-Layout

To convey distrust and a fractured world, the team used deep space with a deep focus, a narrow color palette, higher contrast, heavier film grain, and an arid feel with dust and smoke.

Trust and a united world, on the other hand, were communicated through flat space, with a shallow (broken) focus, a broad color palette, lower contrast, lighter film grain, and a feeling of water with rain and mist.

Various Artists: CG Render

COLOR SCRIPT

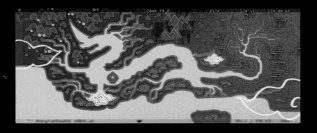

I love doing color keys because a few strokes of color and the right tonality can really give a sense of what the finished film could look like. For Raya and the Last Dragon, we really wanted to communicate that sense early on. So, after establishing a preliminary color script that showed the various times of day and the general pacing of color throughout the film, I tried to have some rough keys done before each story sequence went into production. These were done over beautifully drawn storyboard panels in consultation with Adolph Lusinsky and Rob Dressel, our directors of cinematography. It was a more front-loaded process than usual, but I think it gave everyone a better idea which direction the ship was going. —**Paul Felix, Production Designer**

Mingjue Helen Chen, Brittney Lee, Griselda Sastrawinata, and Ami Thompson: Digital

COLOR SCRIPT

Paul Felix: Digital

Paul Felix: Digital

SET EXTENSION

Traditionally at Disney Animation, the set extension team handles skies and mountains. But in Raya and the Last Dragon, our talented artists took on the creation of entire sets, epic structures, landmarks, and locations by applying a generalist skill set. We utilized modeling, lookdev, lighting, rendering, and digital painting to seamlessly integrate set extension within all departments. It's a "two-and-a-half-D" form of working that saves us a lot of time and resources for one-off and multiple sequence shots because our artists can do the work of many departments all at once. We're affectionately known as the "get it done" team.
—**Adil Mustafabekov, Set Extension Supervisor**

(previous spread) **Various Artists:** CG Render

Adil Mustafabekov, Alex Garcia, Michael Morris, and Travis Mangaoang: Digital

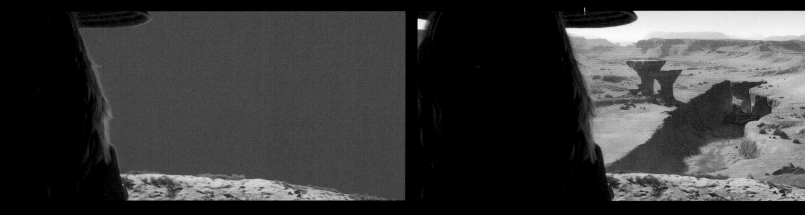

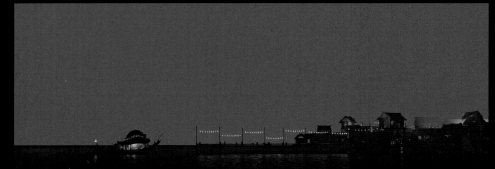

A WORLD OF COLLABORATION

Brandon Batten, Andrew Piccone, and Scott Sakamoto

Everything begins with research and grows into a continuous voyage of learning, from dance demonstrations to a powerful, traditional Baci ceremony for the whole crew performed at the start of production by elders of the Lao community. —**Osnat Shurer, Producer**

It was a tremendous honor to host the Raya *team during their research trip in our village of Pengosekan in Bali at our Karya Ageng Pura Dalem. We continued to work with them at Disney Animation in Burbank, where we spent time with the crew and taught them* kecak *and* gamelan. *Together, we collaborated to find nuance for the characters' movements, even down to how they would take off their shoes before entering a sacred space and how they might communicate through eye contact in a scene.*

—Emiko Saraswati Susilo and I Dewa Putu Berata, Çudamani, Southeast Asia Story Trust

Paul Briggs: Digital

Paul Briggs: Digital

Paul Briggs: Digital

Shiyoon Kim: Digital

Paul Briggs: Digital

James Finch: Digital

Paul Briggs by Paul Felix: Digital

Drawing is my first love. I can't imagine not drawing. I look at it like being a shark. In order to breathe, sharks have to keep swimming. I feel the same way about drawing. **—Don Hall, Director**

Don Hall by Malcon Pierce: Digital

David Derrick and Luis Logam by Allen Ostergar: Digital

Osnat Shurer by Allen Ostergar: Digital

James Romo by Paul Felix: Digital

Fawn Veerasunthorn by Luis Logam: Digital

Qui Nguyen, Osnat Shurer, Scott Sakamoto, Fawn Veerasunthorn, and Shannon Henley by Allen Ostergar: Digital

Carlos López Estrada by Allen Ostergar: Digital

It's quite humbling to be surrounded by so many talented artists. I could honestly frame any meeting doodle from anyone in our crew. Everyone is always doodling. —**Carlos López Estrada, Director**

David VanTuyle by Allen Ostergar: Digital

Adele Lim by Allen Ostergar: Digital

END CREDITS

I've always loved the unique art that accompanies end credits on Disney Animation films. I knew our film deserved a similarly exceptional last statement. As a jumping-off point, I leveraged the artistic style of the Dragon Scroll and worked with head of story Fawn Veerasunthorn and the story team to extend the tale of our heroes after our film. Together with visual development artist April Liu and art director of characters Ami Thompson, we completed all of the art for this sequence in under two weeks! It was truly a labor of love and a perfect way to wrap up my experience on Raya and the Last Dragon. **—Mingjue Helen Chen, Production Designer**

(previous spread) **Various Artists:** CG Render

Mingjue Helen Chen, April Liu, and Ami Thompson: Digital

Mingjue Helen Chen, April Liu, and Ami Thompson: Digital

ACKNOWLEDGMENTS

THE AUTHORS wish to express their sincerest gratitude to Don Hall, Carlos López Estrada, Paul Briggs, and John Ripa for the honor of sharing the story behind *Raya and the Last Dragon*'s visual development from idea to screen.

Thank you to the indomitable Mingjue Helen Chen and Paul Felix for contributing your artistry to the design of this book. We are indebted to you. Cory Loftis, Shiyoon Kim, Ami Thompson, and every artist who took the time to share your creative thought process with us—you poured your heart, soul, and extraordinary talent into this film, and it shows.

While the primary focus of this book is on visual development, we tried to include work from other parts of the pipeline wherever possible. We cannot express enough appreciation for the whole *Raya and the Last Dragon* crew. We'd especially like to thank the production management team, particularly Thai Bettistea, Brittany Kikuchi, Blair Bradley, Aisha Rupasingha, Vanita Borwankar, Kristin Yadamec, Scott Sakamoto, and Elise Aliberti. We are so lucky to work alongside you.

Alison Giordano, we'd be lost without you. Thank you to our editor, Brittany McInerney, for your patience and editorial guidance, and to our book designers Neil Egan and Jennifer Redding for helping us create a stunning visual story. And thank you to Jackson Kaplan and Andrew Elmers for all of your hard work.

On a personal note, Osnat thanks everyone who has made this wonderful journey with us, especially our incredible Southeast Asia Story Trust. Dr. S. Steve Arounsack, Emiko Saraswati Susilo, I Dewa Puta Berata, Nathakrit Tatan Sunthareerat, and Jes Vu, your kindness and guidance made all the difference. Most of all, Osnat thanks Gina for sharing this life with her. Kalikolehua thanks Osnat and Amy Astley for believing in her from the very beginning, Mom for answering every one of her early-morning phone calls, and Chase for picking up their takeout on many late nights during the writing of this book.

—Osnat Shurer and Kalikolehua Hurley

Mingjue Helen Chen: Digital

Ami Thompson: Digital